ABANDONED SALTON SEA

DYSTOPIAN PANORAMAS

CINDY VASKO

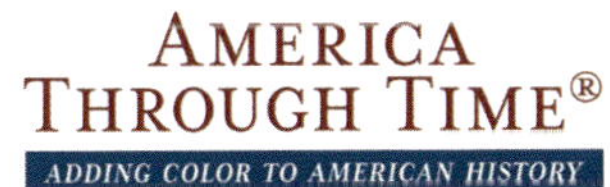
AMERICA THROUGH TIME®
ADDING COLOR TO AMERICAN HISTORY

How we embrace the environment is gingerly interlaced, not just with our existence but with who we are as a people. I dedicate this book to those that find the fortitude and initiative to spotlight the Salton Sea's ecological distress call. Appreciation also goes to Keith Skelton—California Photography Workshops, who provided a profound and enjoyable tumble into the Salton Sea skeleton in California's closet.

America Through Time is an imprint of Fonthill Media LLC
www.through-time.com
office@through-time.com

Published by Arcadia Publishing by arrangement with Fonthill Media LLC
For all general information, please contact Arcadia Publishing:
Telephone: 843-853-2070
Fax: 843-853-0044
E-mail: sales@arcadiapublishing.com
For customer service and orders:
Toll-Free 1-888-313-2665

www.arcadiapublishing.com

First published 2022

ISBN 978-1-63499-377-7

Typeset in Trade Gothic LT Std
Printed and bound in England

CONTENTS

ABOUT THE AUTHOR

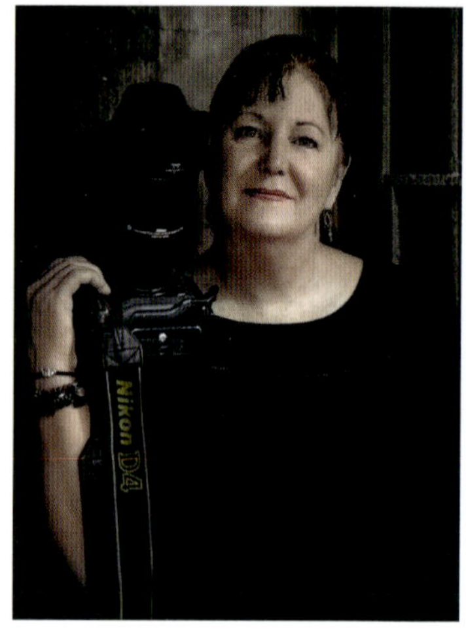

Cindy Vasko was born in Allentown, Pennsylvania, and resides in Arlington, Virginia, near Washington, D.C. For fifteen years, Cindy was the publications manager for a large construction law firm in Northern Virginia, and concurrently, interviewed musicians, wrote articles, and photographed concerts for a music magazine for four years. While Cindy enjoys partaking in all photography genres and is a multifaceted photographer, she has a passion for abandoned site photography. Cindy is an award-winning photographer, and her works were featured in many gallery exhibitions, including galleries in New York City; Washington, D.C.; Philadelphia, Pennsylvania; and Paris, France.

Cindy's *Abandoned Union* series books include: *Abandoned New York*; *Abandoned Maryland: Lost Legacies*; *Abandoned Western Pennsylvania: Separation from a Proud Heritage*; *Abandoned Catskills: Deserted Playgrounds*; *Abandoned Southern New Jersey: A Bounty of Oddities*; *Abandoned Northern New Jersey: Homage to Lost Dreams*; *Abandoned West Virginia: Crumbling Vignettes*; *Abandoned Washington, D.C.: Evanescent Chronicles*; *Abandoned Eastern Ohio: Traces of Fading History*; *Abandoned Eastern Pennsylvania: Remnants of History; Abandoned Southern Virginia: Reckless Surrender*; and coming soon, *Abandoned Northern Virginia: Desolate Beauty.*

INTRODUCTION

Embracing Southern California's Salton Sea ("Sea") for the first time is a surreal experience—the landscape is at once unfamiliar, dramatic, silent, and dystopian. Of course, the Sea's desolation and devastation appeal to my inner urban explorer. I am drawn to peculiar sites that showcase the detritus of departed people and feature nature's hand at the ready for another claim of forsaken space. Like all abandonments I visit and photograph, I see the beauty in the decay. Still, I also discern the short-sighted motivations and wastefulness of societal dynamics leading to such forlornness and the resulting negative consequences that shatter too many dreams and livelihoods.

All of us are fascinated by the perception of a hidden story, and there are thousands of veiled tales of loss tucked into Salton Sea's ghost region. Nature's hand often hurts and reminds all to not forget about this territory and take prompt steps to mitigate the escalating ecological damage. Nevertheless, Dame Nature still manifests technicolor displays of spectacular sunsets and sunrises within the Sea's domain—as if it is her duty to open her paint box and decorate the sky each morning and evening with a riot of color and overcompensate for the manufactured Sea mishap. The Sea landscape, therefore, is a study in contrast with so much atmospheric vibrancy coupled with *memento mori*—dangerous beauty in an apocalyptic-like wonderland. Is the Sea forever held hostage within a sealed, doomed fate? Can the Sea be salvaged?

The Sea was not always an environmental horror. To understand the enchantment and allure of this province, however, one must know the story about the notorious calamity known as the Salton Sea. The Sea is actually a lake—an accidental reservoir that assumed thriving beach districts in the 1950s and 1960s and held monikers such as the Riviera of the West and Miracle in the Desert. At this time, the Sea brought forth one-half million annual visits—more than Yosemite National Park. The mid-century era featured coastlines of yacht clubs, marinas, and beachfront communities. So many flocked to the area for fishing, waterskiing, boating, golfing, and entertainment. Hollywood icons, such as Frank Sinatra, Jerry Lewis, Marx Brothers, and the Beach Boys, undertook pilgrimages to the Sea for a grab of the aquatic gifts. Shore property was a hot commodity, too, as people clamored to clutch a slice of sunshiny paradise for a weekend getaway or settle in as full-time residents within this fashioned nirvana. In the 1950s, the California Department of Fish and Game stocked the Sea with various fish species for the promotion of sport fishing. The Sea quickly advanced as a popular and revered angling site. In the 1970s, however, California's Riviera transformed into a wasteland of devastation. With Tropical Storms Kathleen and Doreen sweeping through the locale and above-average rainfall battering the region for years afterward, along with increased agricultural run-off from the Imperial Valley farming community, the shoreline enclaves flooded and enveloped the destruction of hundreds of homes and businesses. Sea residents abandoned the zone in a mass exodus, and the sector assumed the new hat of ecological disaster. Eventually, the environment that once battled too much water thirsted for an assuagement of its parched shores and, to this day, still squawks this alarm. The Sea is a growing toxic danger with its continuous shrinking field of water exposing a cocktail of salts and chemicals whipped into menacing airborne swells that impact the health of many, including those far from the Sea's Imperial and Riverside counties.

This Sea's geography emerged 10,000 years ago with the formation of the Salton Sink. The Salton Sink is the lowest point of the Endorheic basin and does not offer water outflow to other tracts in the Sonoran Desert. The Sea roots, though, originated in actions occurring in 1905—the beginning of its end. In 1901, the California Development Company recognized the richness of California's Imperial Valley's soil and the prospects for a productive agricultural arena. Accordingly, irrigation canals from the Colorado River to the old Alamo River channel were constructed and generated over 100,000 acres of fertile farmland. Thousands flocked to the area to partake in fruitful farming endeavors. Within a few years, however, heavy silt accumulated in the canals and restricted the accessibility of irrigation water for crops. Consequently, the decision to create a fissure in the western bank of the Colorado River to allow additional water to flow to the Imperial Valley was set in motion. Unfortunately, the severe water pressure on the bank's split generated a large bank breach and allowed the Colorado River's water to gush beyond the Sea irrigation canals and flood the Imperial Valley's dry Salton Sink. The uncontrolled

Colorado River water discharged into the Salton Sink for two years—hence, the formation of the Salton Sea. Since much farmland seeded the region prior to the river breach, the flooding destroyed these agricultural fields.

Before the Colorado River flooded the Salton Sink, the Southern Pacific Railroad brought forth designs for the creation of the Imperial Valley rail line. Of course, the Railroad's construction plans derailed with the flooding. To dam the Colorado River's surge into the Imperial Valley, Southern Pacific built a train trestle over the flooded land and delivered train cars filled with rock and other debris for release into the flooded channels. The railroad's efforts halted the water flow, and the terminal lake called the Salton Sea was the new desert feature. The Sea's water remained and was sustained, in part, by agricultural run-off from the irrigation in the Imperial and Coachella Valleys. Agriculture resumed near the beautiful inland Sea, and decades later, another form of development took root—recreation and tourism.

Since the Sea was originally a freshwater lake, courtesy of the Colorado River, it quickly became an oasis for migrating birds and sport fishing. In the 1950s and 1960s, resorts and residential communities peppered the rim of the Sea—the "Salton Riviera" was in full bloom and attracted millions of visitors and celebrities. Water sports, fishing, swimming, and entertainment were big attractions. Yet, by the 1960s, the Sea's salinity content was higher than the Pacific Ocean and negatively impacted wildlife in and around the Sea.

Further, salts from prehistoric Salton Sink deposits mingled with the agricultural run-off holding salts, pesticides, and fertilizers. Toxic chemicals were held hostage in a basin without an escape due to the Sea's terminal aspect. Over the decades, a continuing rise in salinity and noxiousness commenced an organic holocaust. Much of the fish population died, and numerous avian migrations to the Sea disappeared. Algae blooms were constant and stifled the water's oxygen content, killing even more fish. Instead of sand, the Sea beaches hold deep layers of bleached, pulverized fish bones. Palm trees struggle to survive, and dead trees dot the landscape, but many lifeless trees refuse to crumble as if to remind all of humanity's destructive hand—monuments to failed dreams and ruin. The more the Sea basin is exposed, the deadlier it is. Winds pick up the polluted dust and carry it as far north as Los Angeles. Asthma and respiratory issues abound.

The place, in many respects, is uninhabitable. The region's tattered appearance accelerates with the salt and chemical-filled air, courtesy of the evaporating Sea. Even for a seasoned urban explorer like myself, it is heartrending to see so much abandonment and shuttered vestiges of what was once a happy and promising era. Nevertheless, it is crucial to witness such destruction and realize the environmental consequences of thoughtless and short-sighted engagements. The tangible forms of regret are front and center everywhere—sun-weathered real estate signs, boarded businesses, home husks, sunken trailers, beaches bearing an amalgamation of cast-off personal treasures, construction materials, and annihilated fish and bird bones. This accidental man-made predicament is wholly in the clutch of a creeping ecological quandary affecting a vast and growing swath of the United States and Mexico. The Sea region is, in effect, a war zone with compounding negative environmental impacts that will soon present a point of no return unless serious attention and funding migrate toward a resolution of this rolling menace.

1

NATURE'S MIRAGE: EAST SHORES

Highway 111 grips the shoreline along the east side of the often-visible Salton Sea between Mecca and Niland. Towns sprouted along the coastline during the 1940s-1960s. Still, with variable sea levels and a multitude of major storms in the 1970s, the resultant regional destruction compelled a massive population flight from the east side. The once idyllic and short-lived recreational destinations are now settings of desolation. The ghost-like east flank reveals a throng of skeletal homes and businesses along 111. The shoreline exposes carpets of tumbled fish bones holding rooted building materials, fragments of derelict boats anchored in chemical sludge surrounded by a mish-mash of debris, dense biochemical crusts at the water's edge, and at times, water displaying non-organic colors.

I visited the Sea during the winter to avoid the searing temperatures and notorious nauseating fish smell that shrouds the beaches. My first Sea stop was the Mecca Beach Campground facility. After a glance at the neglected and weedy campsite and its sun-weathered picnic tables and canopies, one's eye affixes on a perceived wonder of nature—the Sea. Deep azure water is colored in part by the reflection of the glorious sapphire sky. The Sea joins a dazzling, blinding white beach for a dramatic visual contrast. The backdrop of the peach and purple-hued San Jacinto mountains seals this perfect composition. As a bonus, the graceful glide of gulls, just inches above the water, soared across the Sea, and in the near distance, a squadron of snow-white pelicans hugged a narrow sandbar. My friend and I shared this splendor without the presence of another soul at Mecca Beach, and we coveted nature's chirpy harmonies echoing in such a rare environment. Nature's glory, yes? No, more like an idealized mirage. We were still standing on the macadam campground parking lot with an outward gaze and at quite a distance from the shore's edge and the sandbars that hosted the pelicans and other birds. We had yet to have our first up close and personal Sea beach experience.

The long view is sublime, but a macro examination of the Sea's ecosystem unveils disturbing truths. Does not one anticipate the cushiony feeling of sand with the first step on a beach? On the contrary, Mecca Beach's "sand" delivers a hard crunch with a footstep—akin to stepping on ice-crusted snow. Of course, this sensation prompts an examination of the substance underfoot. The reality is that the beach is not sand covered and, instead, blanketed with voluminous layers of millions of minced sun-bleached fish bones, barnacles, and agricultural chemical run-off accumulations. Almost immediately, one meets a brown fish skeleton on top of the remains, and then another and another. It is difficult to walk along the water's edge, because the Sea's salt content forms sharp, jagged chemical-laden formations. In addition, the water along the shore edge is foamy and opaque—parts of the water are green, while other parts are yellow, brown, or red, and hold a multitude of foreign particulate—certainly not an invitation for swimming or even dipping a toe into this "substance."

It was challenging to walk along the bone beach, but I wanted a better view of the beauteous American White Pelicans. I noticed a few brown pelicans mingled within the party mix, too. Being present at this moment was a fortunate opportunity to witness these birds *en masse*, because White Pelicans are among the fastest disappearing Sea species. In 2008, the Sea hosted 20,000 pelicans, but fewer than 100 remained in 2019. The pelican decline is attributed to the Sea's vanishing Tilapia stock due to increasing Sea salinity, Type C Botulism and avian viruses. Tilapia is the primary food source for the American White Pelican in this region. At one time, the Sea's eastern rim held the annual Pelican Day Birding Festival. Now, there are so few pelicans in the area, and it is heartbreaking to confront another one of Mother Nature's Sea casualties.

As I approached the pelicans, one could hear their loud gabbling, as if this pod of feathered creatures was engaging in a political debate. At first, the pelicans did not see two humans approaching their narrow sandbar, but then they started to cautiously move north along the shoal, in lockstep and without a break in their prattle. The movement prompted a few pelicans to leave the feathered clique and take flight. We did not want to disturb the pelicans' tranquility once the pod reached the tip of the sandbar, so we halted our advance. I attached my long lens to my camera body and grabbed a few images of the handsome troop. I knew I probably would not ever see such a splendid gathering again. I also saw a few Black-Necked Stilts on some smaller sandbars, and one even balanced on a beer can. I still marvel at my long-view images of the shoreline, mountains, and crystal blue water and want this area to return to this flawless idealized state—this sphere is so worthy of a fix.

My next stop was the east side's dystopian-esque Bombay Beach. In the 1950s and 1960s, Bombay Beach was a booming resort town and offered swimming, waterskiing, boating, and golfing. Imagining this model of leisure is difficult when one observes today's Bombay Beach. Stepping upon the beach is even a strange occurrence—a high berm surrounds the shoreline and obscures the beach view from the town.

As an urban explorer, I find Bombay Beach very alluring with its endless tales of past glory in contrast to its present decay. I see the beauty in the deterioration and the need for remembrance, along with a requisite embrace of its cautionary environmental tale. Unfortunately, the town of Bombay Beach is silent and on the verge of ghost-town status. Bombay Beach's population is under 300, and the numbers have not budged since 2010. The town does not have a gas station or even a grocery store except for a sparsely supplied convenience store, but it has a bar. The nearest hospital requires a forty-five-minute journey, and one has to drive to Niland for gas, twenty miles away. The Bombay Beach town landscape is peppered with boarded or windowless shells of homes and trailers with most of these vacancies adorned with graffiti. I only saw a few people wandering along the beach and did not see anyone out and about on the residential streets.

Bombay Beach emerged as a small private community in 1929 but quickly grew by the 1960s due to the Sea's recreational offerings. Fish angler's flocked to Bombay Beach for the abundant Corvina swelling to thirty pounds. The fish lured the bird migrations to the area, and a bourgeoning ecological habitat formed. Hollywood celebrities promoted the appeal of Bombay Beach, and Californians funneled to the site on weekends.

The 1970s, though, brought forth repeated devastating tropical storms that flooded and destroyed many town structures. In addition to development short-sightedness, repeated flooding sealed the fate of this modern-day disaster. Because Bombay Beach is one of the lowest elevations in the United States at 227 feet below sea level, its natural geography held the flood water hostage. Shortly thereafter, the reduction of water flowing into the Sea and its subsequent evaporation generated a hyper-saline state for the remaining water. Since 2003, this attribute has exterminated more than three dozen fish species that once claimed the Sea as home. With each passing year, more birds disappear from the landscape. Chemical slurries bubble at the shoreline, and algae blooms abound. The barren landscape appears lifeless and is a baneful vision with artifacts littering the beach. Bombay Beach décor includes wooden frames of former businesses and homes, tires, shoes, boots, a piano, furniture, toilets, outboard motorboats, and even a massive rusty, brine-crusted construction crane that appeared ready to wreak havoc on the community, akin to the dirt-mover in the cult 1970s movie, Killdozer. In essence, if one does not know the history of the Salton Sea, the Bombay Beach environment looks like a war casualty. Still, Mother Nature gifts the scene with the grand Chocolate Mountains as a backdrop and commands remarkable sunrise and sunset panoramas, as if reminding the universe that splendor remains and nature's grandeur rules. As in Mecca Beach, one easily focuses on the colorful skies and mountain ranges, especially at sunrise and sunset, and overlooks man's folly if only for a few minutes with the morning and nightly rollouts of nature's mirages.

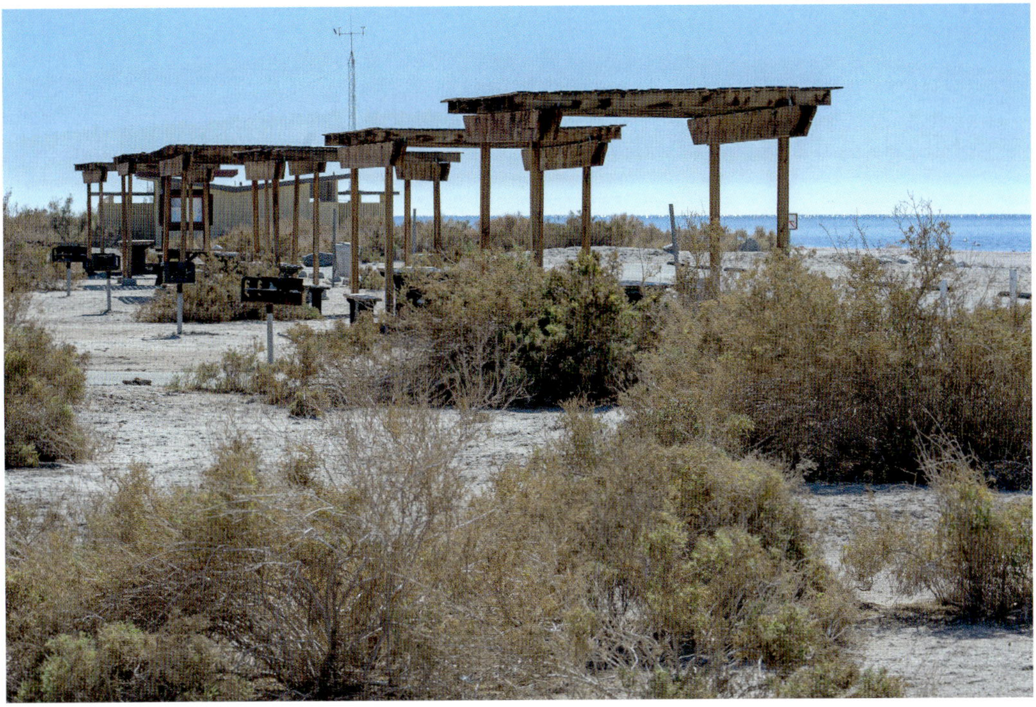

MECCA BEACH CAMPGROUND: A few weathered picnic tables, canopies, fire rings, and RV hookups at the Mecca Beach Campsite.

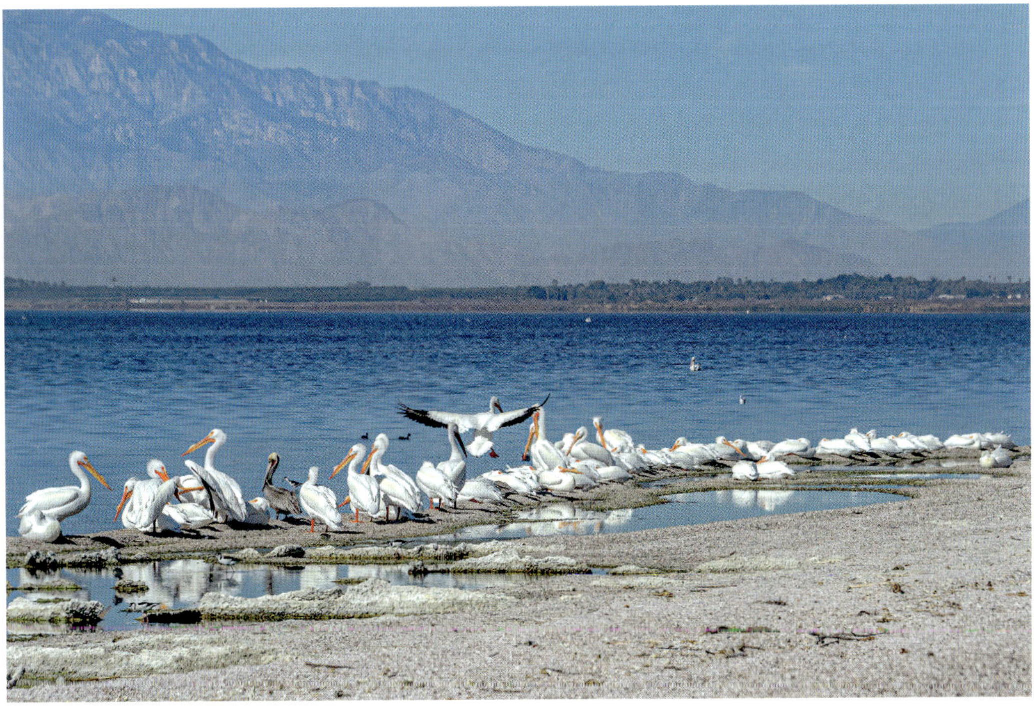

AMERICAN WHITE PELICANS ON SANDBAR: Mecca Beach is on the northeast side of the Salton Sea and is located along Highway 111.

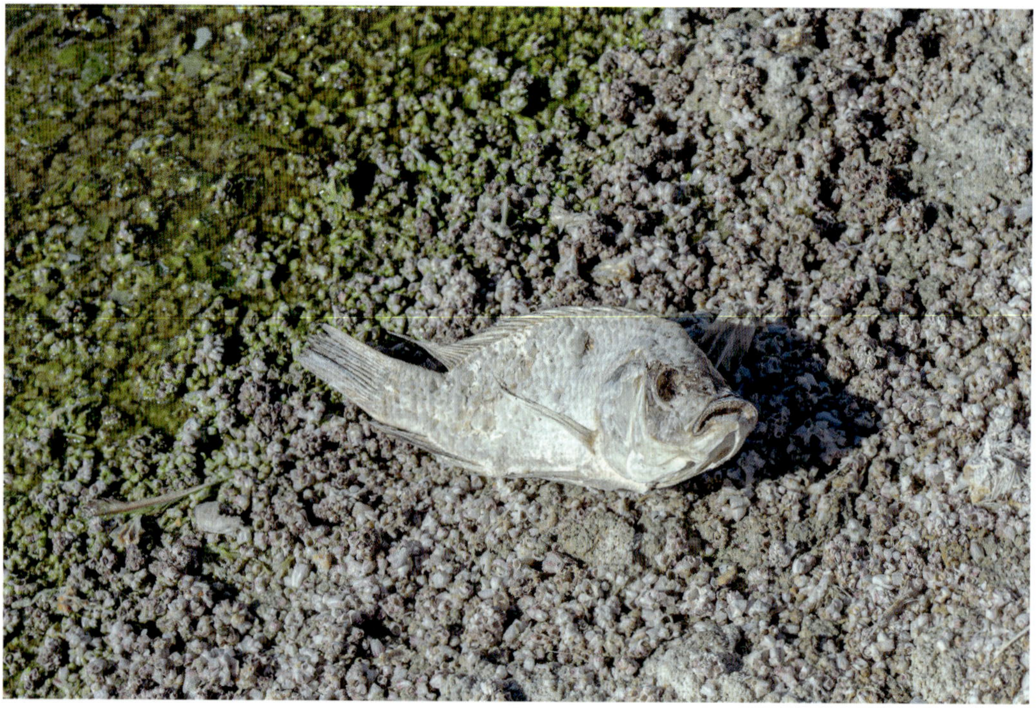

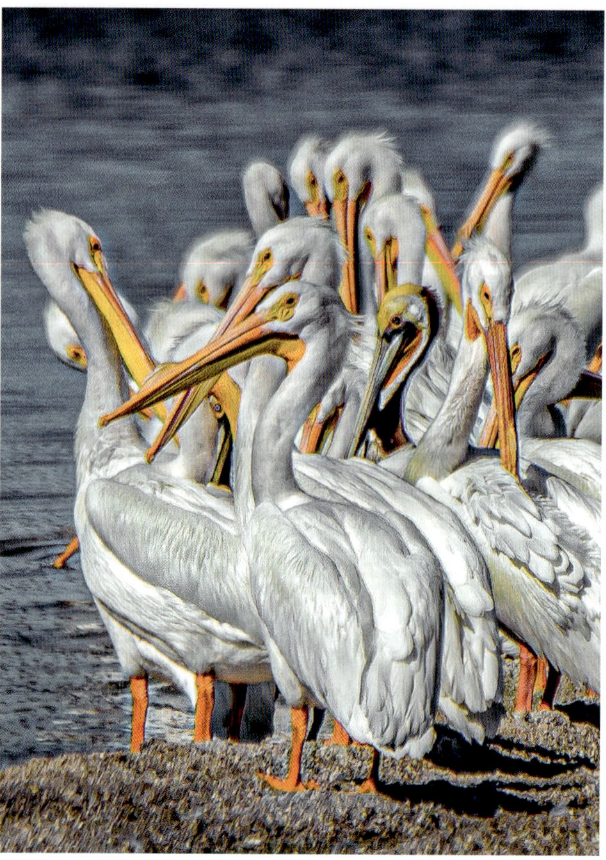

▲ **MECCA BEACH:** The beach is a carpet of fish bones and carcasses.

▼ **PELICANS:** The American White Pelicans of the Salton Sea rely on Tilapia as a food source. The Sea's Tilapia population perished in record numbers within the past few years.

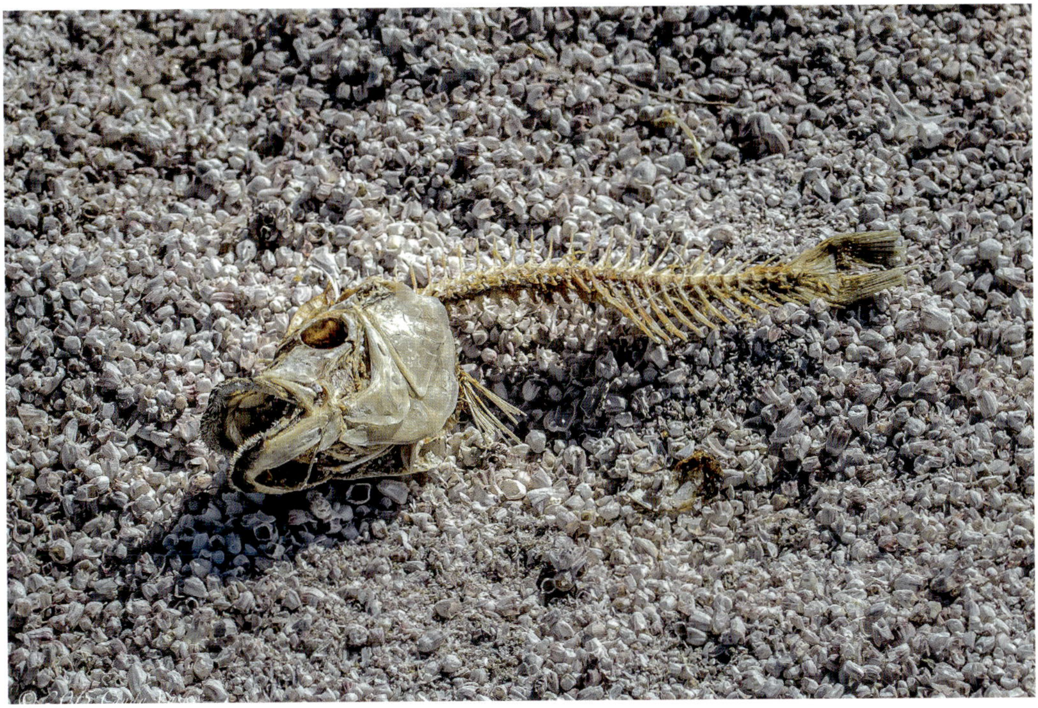

FISH CARCASS: The Salton Sea's escalating salinity imperils the fish populations and hinders reproduction.

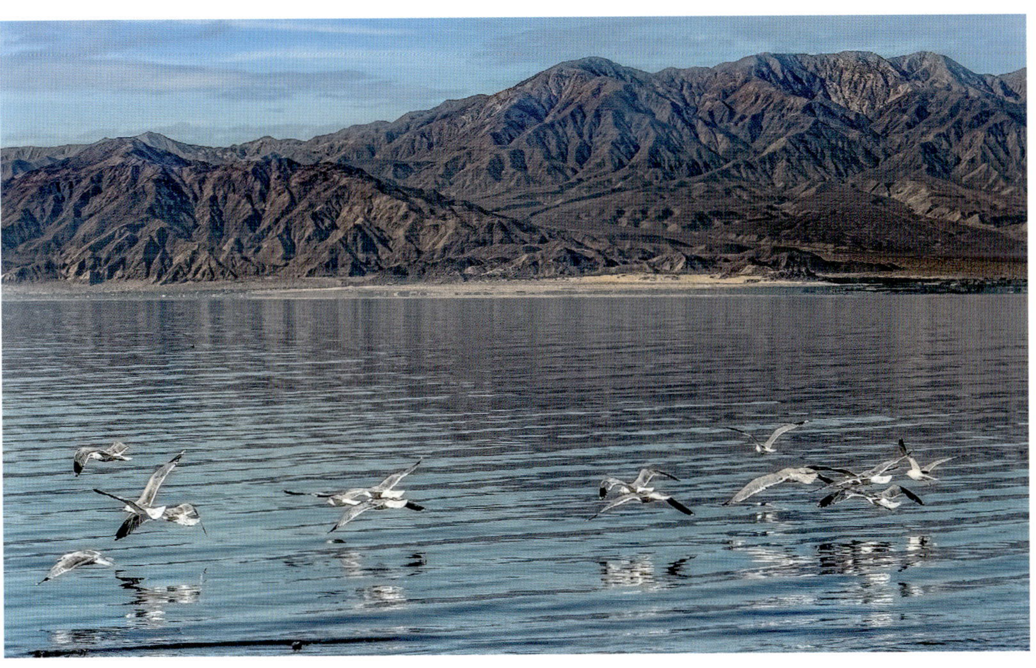

LANDSCAPE: From a distance, Mecca Beach looks like the image of nature's ideal, but a closer examination presents an ecological disaster.

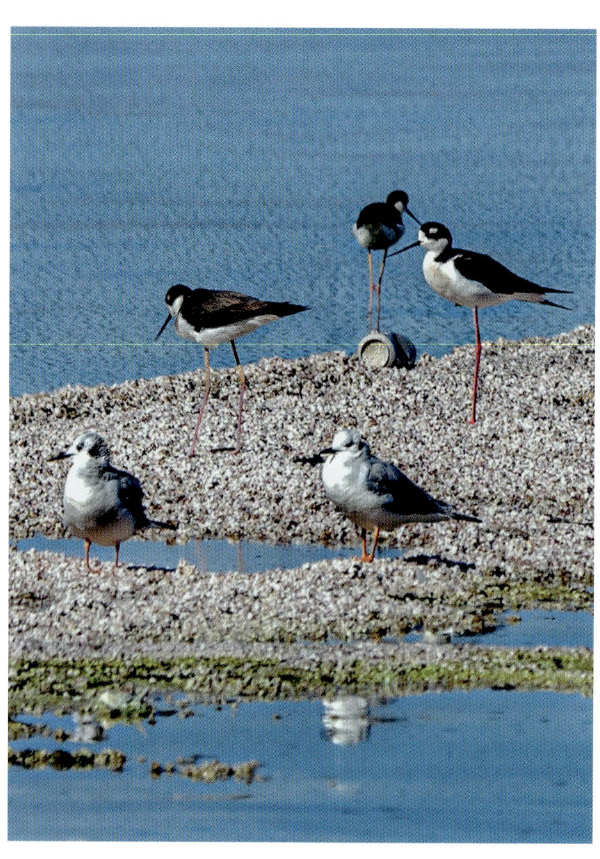

▲ **BLACK-NECKED STILTS ON SANDBAR:** Black-Necked Stilts are usually found in wetlands. In the Salton Sea region, the Stilts forage the beach for food.

▼ **BOMBAY BEACH DOCK REMNANTS:** In the 1950s-1960s, Bombay Beach was a flourishing resort.

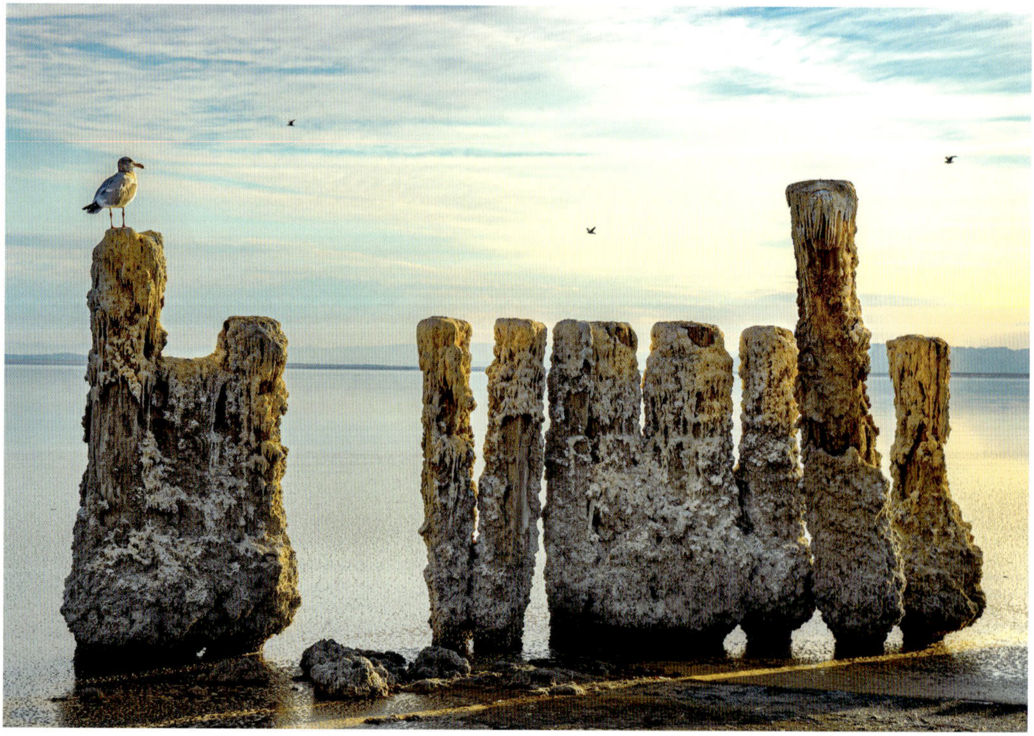

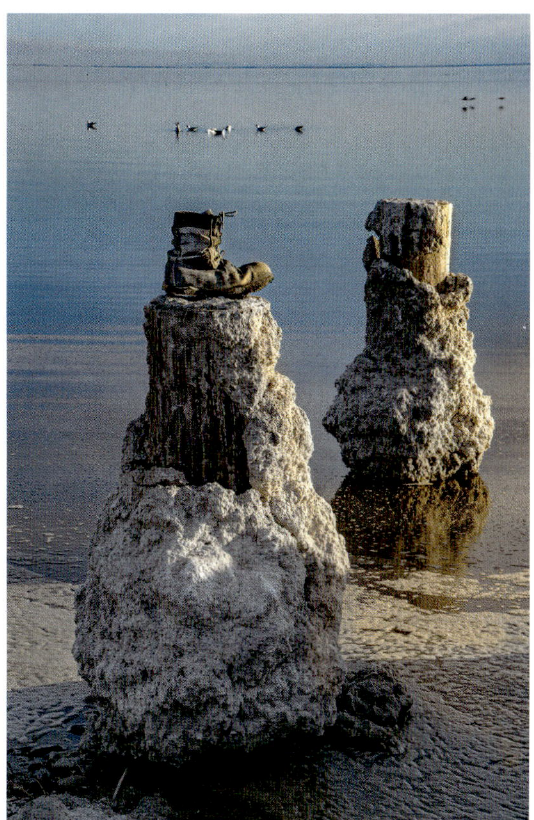

▲ **DOCK PILLARS:** Water-skiing, boating, and swimming were common Bombay Beach daytime recreational activities in the 1950s-1960s. At night, the local yacht club was teeming with partiers.

▼ **SHORELINE RUINS:** Today, Bombay Beach is a desolate, arid wasteland of shattered dreams.

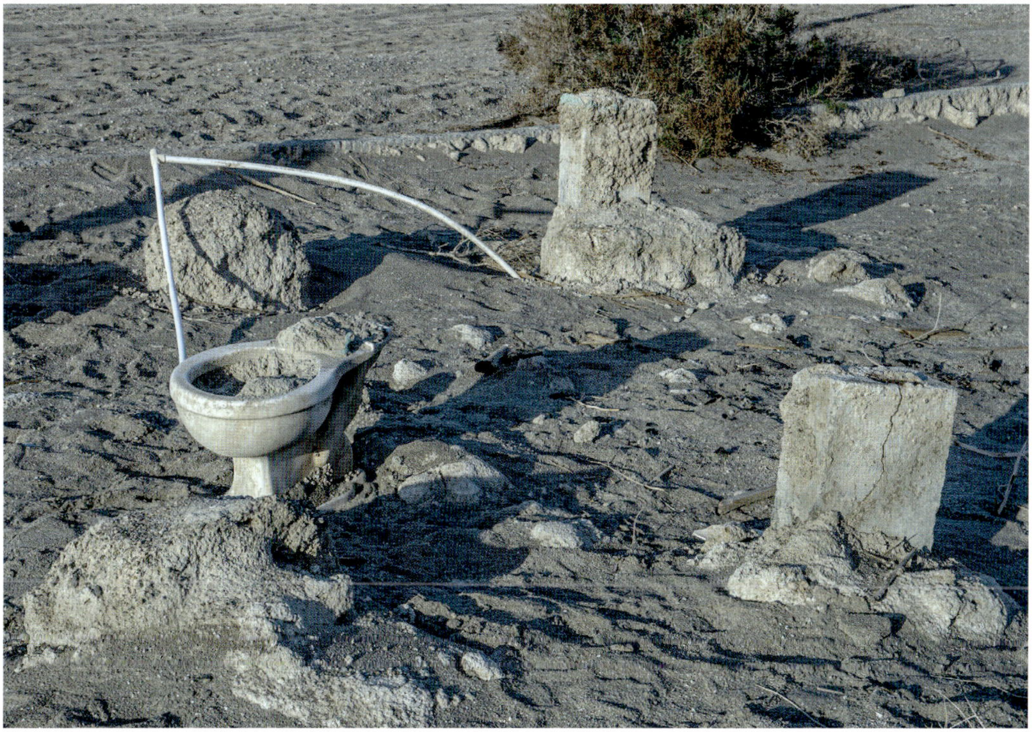

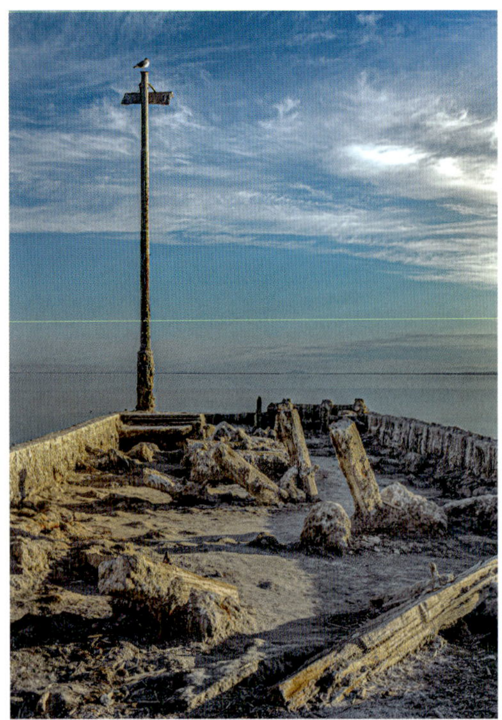

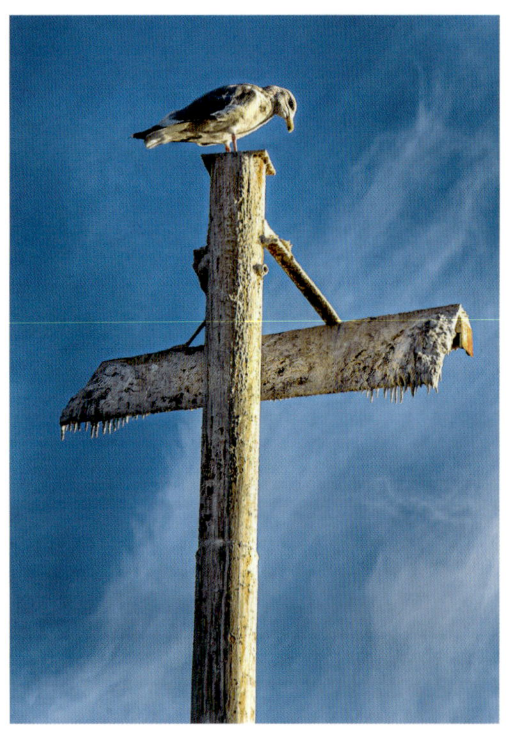

◄ **ABANDONED PIER:** The Salton Sea has no outlet and is a terminal lake, meaning that water can only exit by evaporation, and thus, contributes to the environmental devastation of the region.

► **PIER TOWER:** Salton Sea's rising salinity triggered the extermination of many bird and fish species.

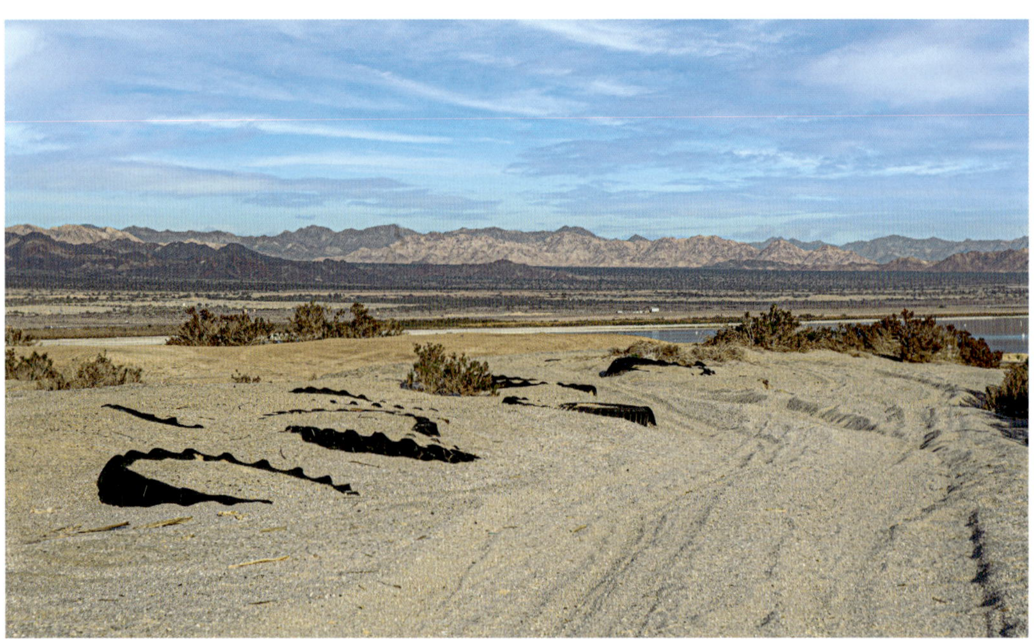

LANDSCAPE: Because of the variable Salton Sea levels, a high berm was constructed to protect Bombay Beach's west side residents.

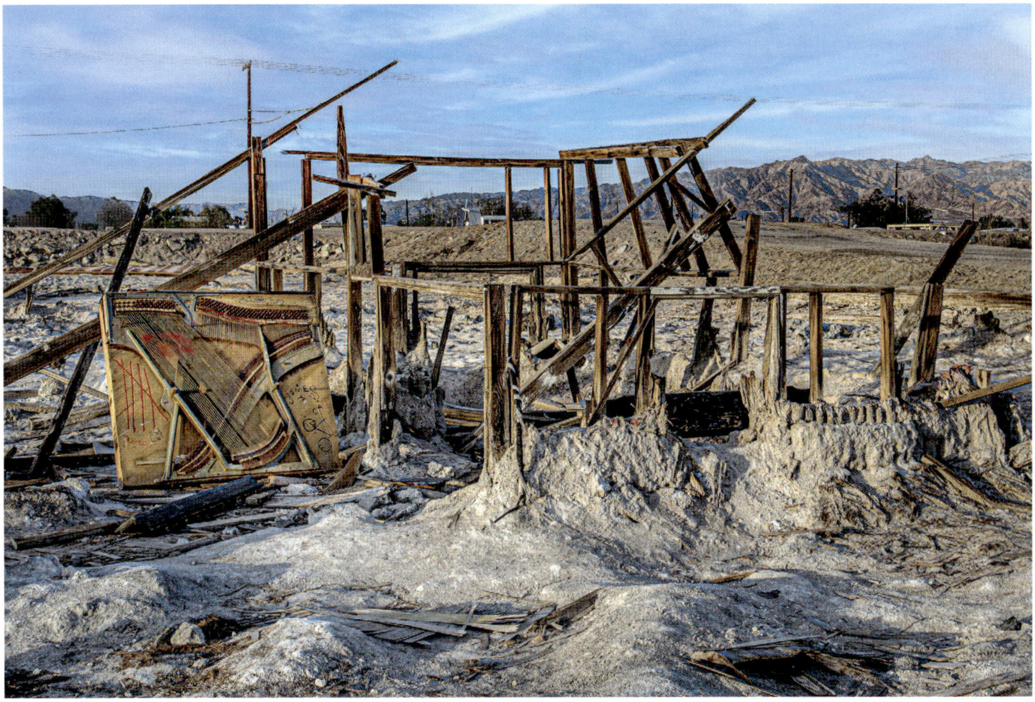

A PIANO AMIDST THE BEACH RUINS: In the 1950s, Bombay Beach was developed as a playground for the affluent and was dubbed the California Riviera.

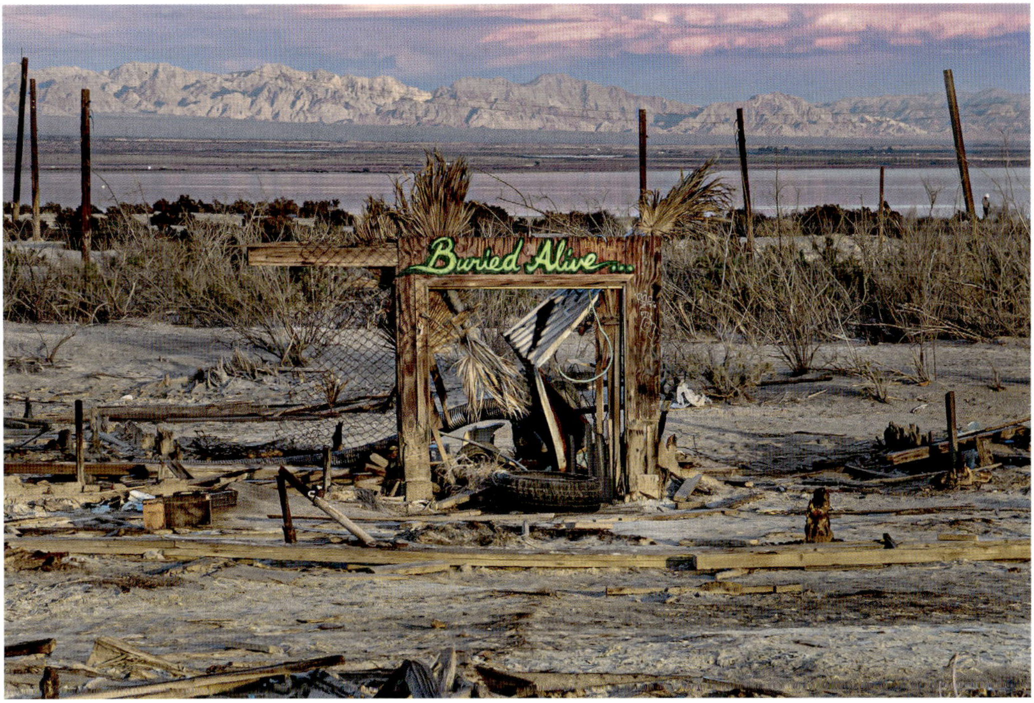

FORMER BUSINESS: Bombay Beach ranks as the second-lowest altitude settlement in North America; Death Valley ranks first with a minimal feet difference.

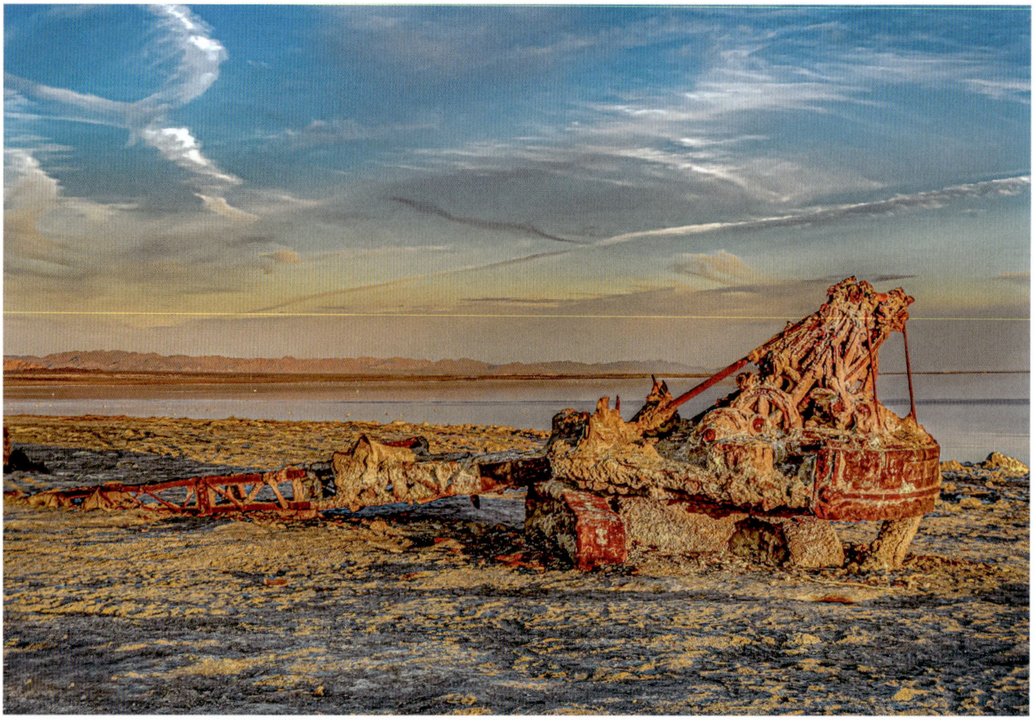

DERELICT CONSTRUCTION CRANE AT GOLDEN HOUR: The setting sun paints a mammoth barnacle and salt-crusted construction crane with golden rays.

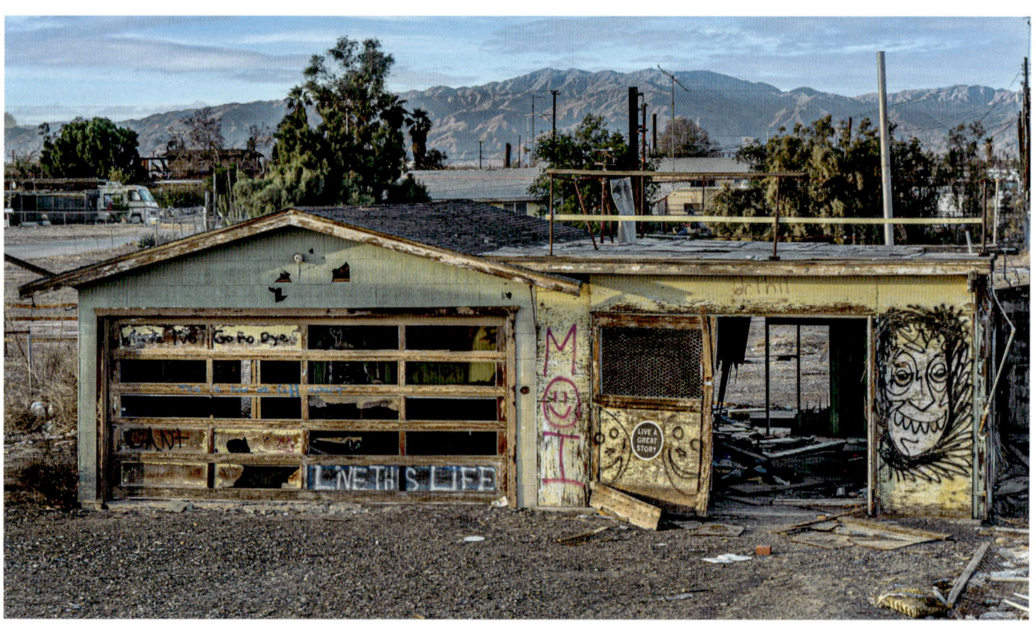

ABANDONED HOME: During the 1970s, Bombay Beach experienced massive flooding and devastation, with a population flight ensuing in the wake.

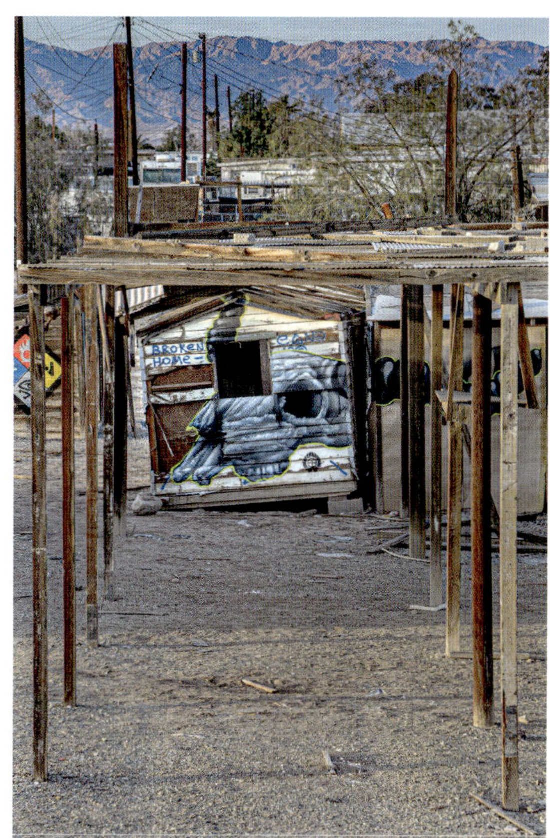

▲ **ABANDONED HOME HUSK:** Bombay Beach was also once referred to as a "Palm Springs with Water."

▼ **PIER RUINS AT SUNSET:** The magnificent colors of sunset on Bombay Beach distract from the ecological danger of the Salton Sea.

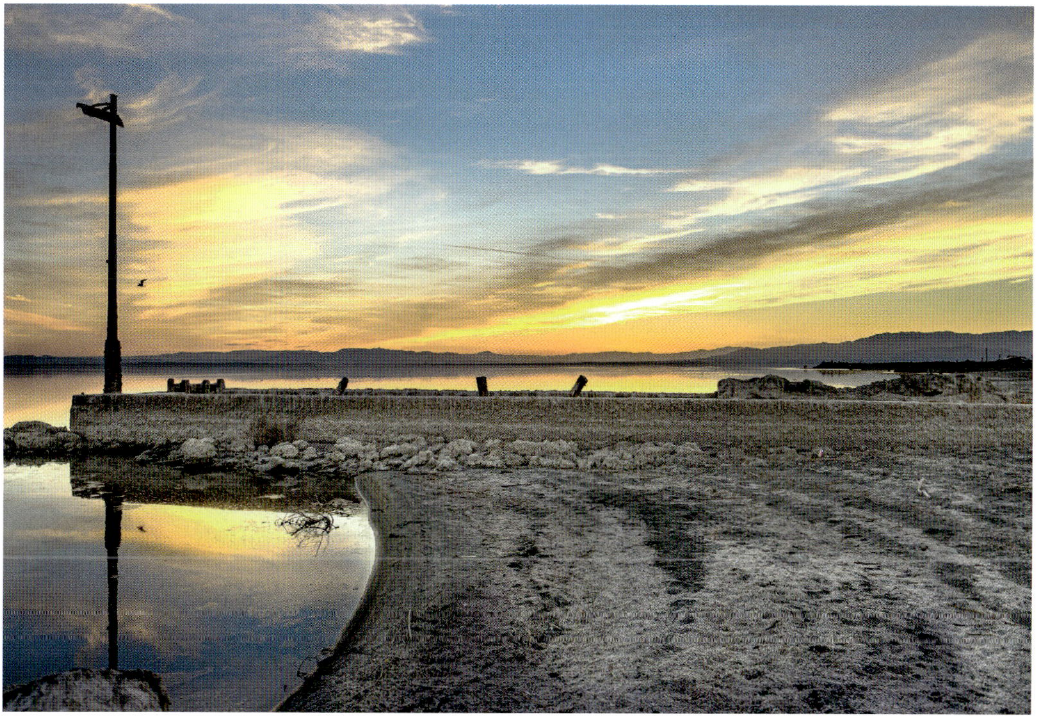

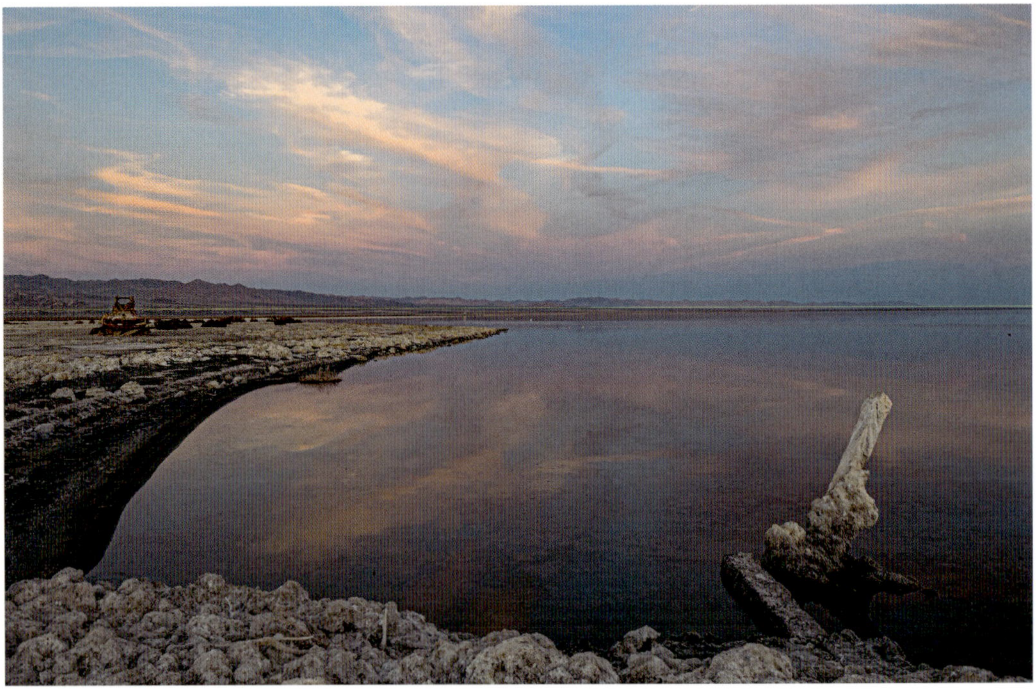

BOMBAY BEACH SUNSET: A sharp and thick chemical crust forms at the edge of the Sea.

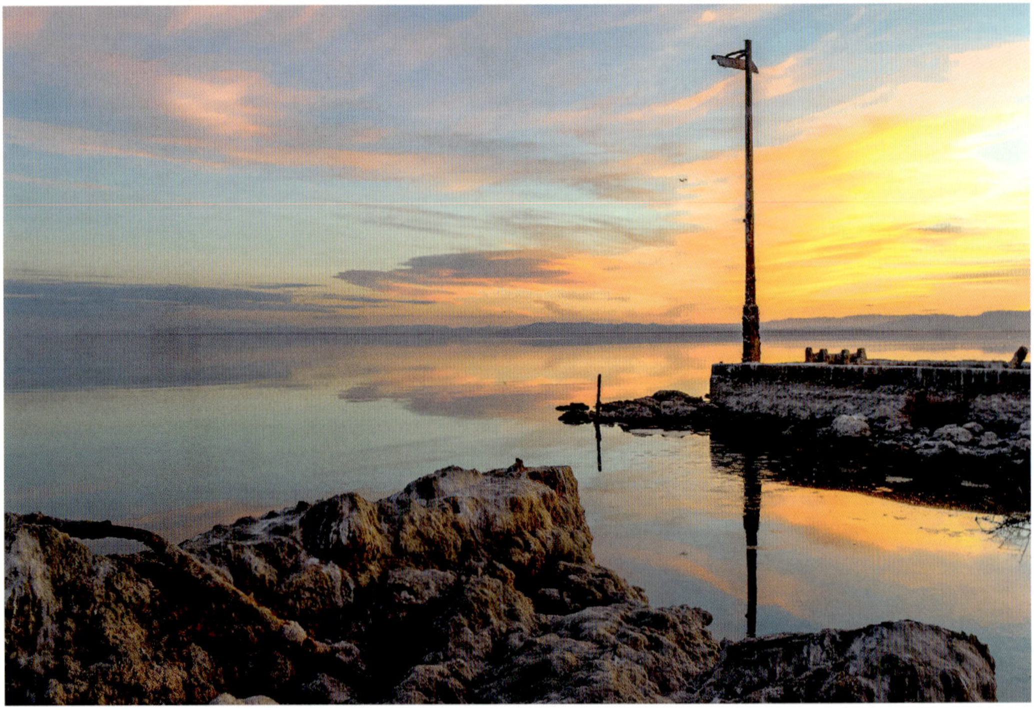

BOMBAY BEACH SUNSET: From afar, the Sea looks like nature's miracle with a sunset explosion of vivid color.

2

LOST DREAMS:
WEST SHORES

Like Salton Sea's east side, the west side also holds a north-south artery, Highway 86. The highway parallels the shoreline, but unlike its east side sister, Highway 111, this thoroughfare does not hug the coast, yet is still only a few miles from shore points. Access to the beach is possible through several towns such as Desert Shores and Salton City. Partially developed resort communities sink and fade into the desert landscape up and down the west coast. One sees so many paved streets and empty parking lots leading to nothingness with continuous vacant lots on each side. Some areas hold scarred and scabbed derelict homes and businesses—mere shells of their former selves. Developers once had high hopes for thriving communities on the west side, too, and offered promises of glorious beachfront getaways. Instead, with the growing Sea environmental problems and limited employment opportunities, isolation and desolation became the order of the day. Like Bombay Beach, the communities serving Salton City and Desert Shores show the wounds of desertion from the harsh decades since the 1970s.

Desert Shores is one of several small coastline towns, and like all Sea towns, has resort development origins in the 1950s. Like its Sea town counterparts, Desert Shores was also a prized fishing spot for Corvina and other game fish. Desert Shores still holds some residents, with several west siders holding employment in the upper Coachella Valley.

An abandoned Desert Shores clubhouse, though, caught my eye. With the clubhouse's back door propped open, I accepted this accessible invitation for a rogue investigation. Once called the Marina Mobile Estates Clubhouse, the site incurred demolition a few years ago. While I poked around the facility, I witnessed a glut of personal mementos, including family photo albums, letters, shoes, movie cassettes, littering the clutter-filled interior—a mass of free association of scraps from multi-lives. Across from the former clubhouse, the fire station presented frayed California and United States flags as if to mock and reflect the sad state of the area.

The west side's Salton City, and its adjoining beachfront, of course, presents a more dismal image of what once was. I saw vast expanses of lots with so much debris strewn about that this section of Salton City also looked like the aftermath of a battle zone. Nothing but hulls and frames of former homes and businesses remained. Garbage, furniture, and pieces of electronics occupied sidewalks to nowhere. Power poles were still present but assumed dangling cut power lines. When the wind kicked up, twirls of dust holding chemical particulate rotated on the empty roads to further aggravate the respiratory problems of this region. Indeed, the Imperial Valley air quality can be so toxic that the Salton City schools hoist red flags as warnings of environmental danger. So many Salton City dreams vanished, but the dust devils continue to breed.

In the 1950s, Salton City's ambitious development originally included 25,000 residential lots with more than 250 miles of paved roads and supporting utilities. Busloads of potential buyers and investors arrived to gawk at the planned communities' wondrous future—a playground of pools, beaches, boat slips, and golf courses. By 1951, 15,000 possessed Salton City property holdings. The community jewel, the Salton Bay Yacht Club, was constructed at the cost of $500,000. Boaters raced across the water, and fishing enthusiasts crowded the Sea for the marine bounties. The Imperial Irrigation District identified Salton City as the "Salton Miracle by the Desert Sea." All indicators pointed to an upward growth arrow for Salton City, but within a decade, reveries shattered. The Sea, prone to variable sea levels, interfered with stable or planned recreational agendas. By the 1970s, hopes and dreams were relegated to the memory plane. The outline of a once grand and manicured tourist parking lot is now cluttered with debris, bordered by dead palm trees, and chipped and peeling concrete curbs and posts.

Like so much in the Imperial Valley, Salton City presents an abandoned appearance, and the section I visited looked like a combination of a ghost town and combat casualty. Nature's hand often assails myopic manufactured vision but always leaves palpable regret in the parochial artificial wake. The evidence of the Sea's intolerant shame is visually all-consuming in a 360-degree fashion.

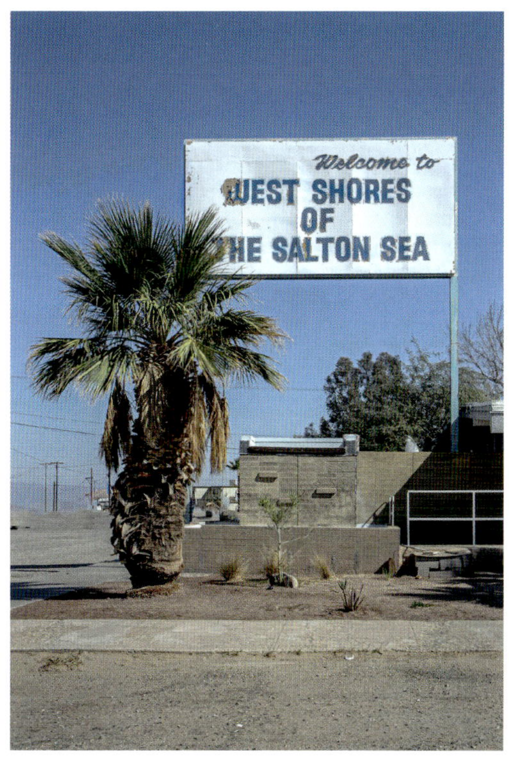

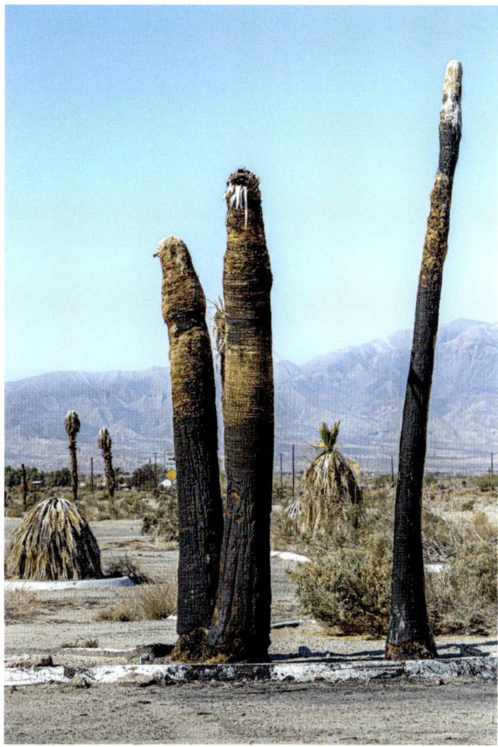

◀ **WEST SHORES:** Salton Sea's partially developed 1960s resort towns continue to crumble into obscurity.

▶ **DESERT SHORES PARKING LOT:** Dead and sickly pine trees dot the once-manicured parking lot that at one time obliged customers to the western Salton Sea.

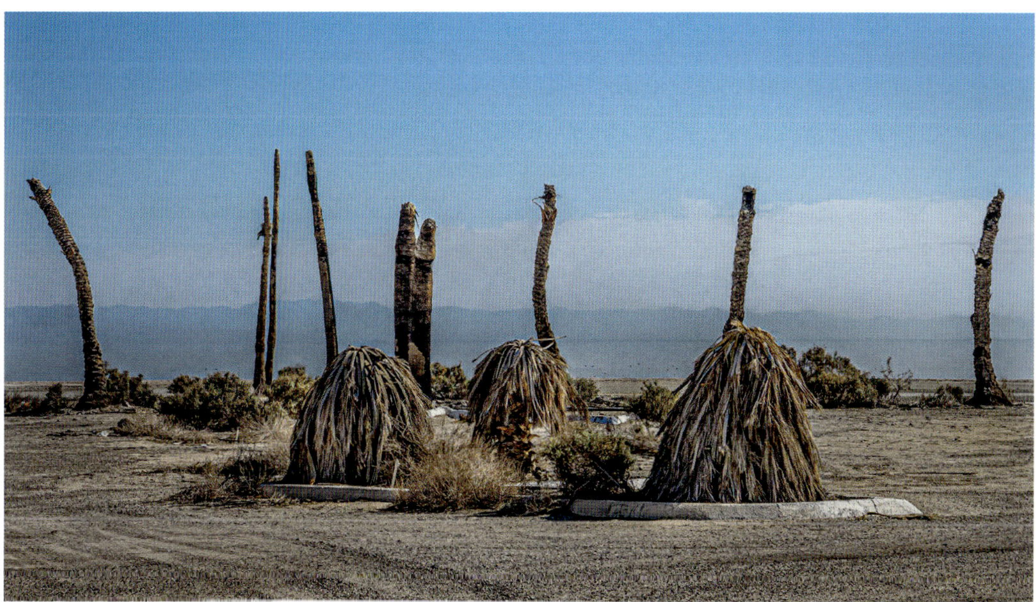

DESERT SHORES PARKING LOT: The large, deserted parking lot on Salton Sea's west side features a plethora of dead and ailing pine trees.

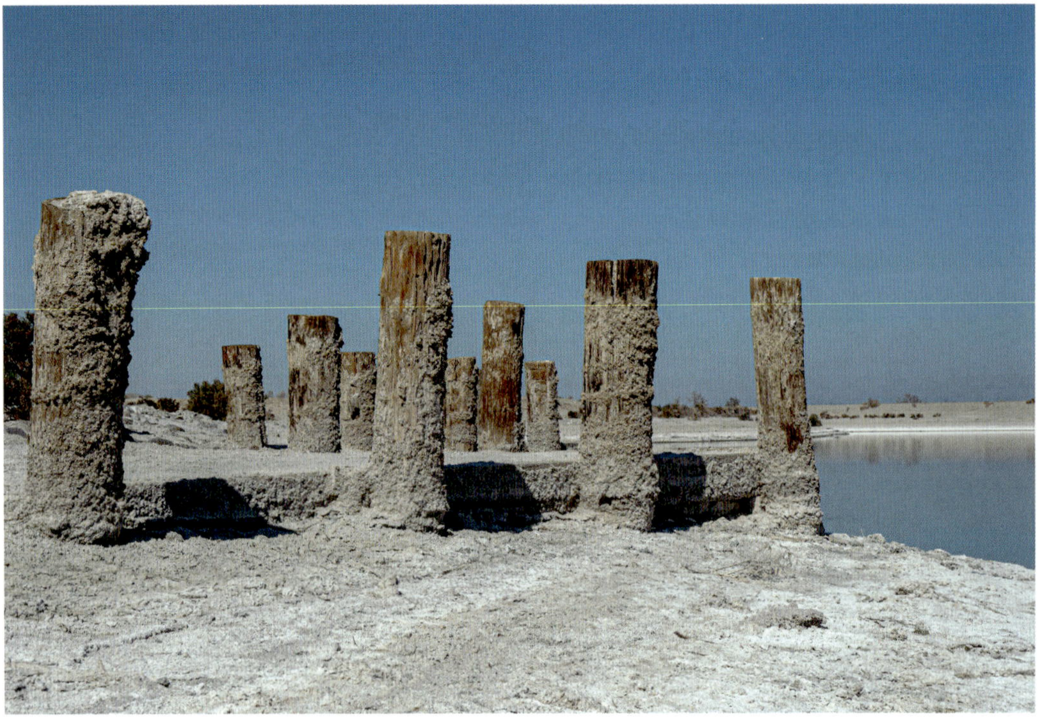

CRUMBLING PIER: Desert Shores is a small community on the west side of the Salton Sea.

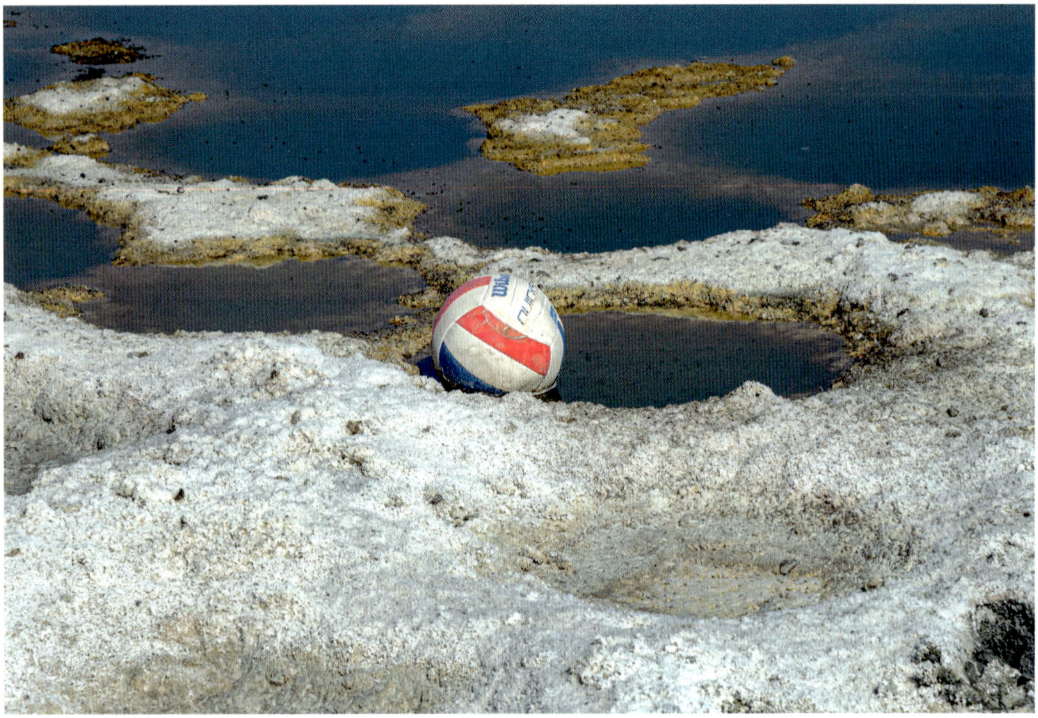

DESERT SHORES COASTLINE: The escalating salinity, Sea evaporation, and agricultural run-off creates ragged chemical scabs amidst pools of variable unnatural water tones.

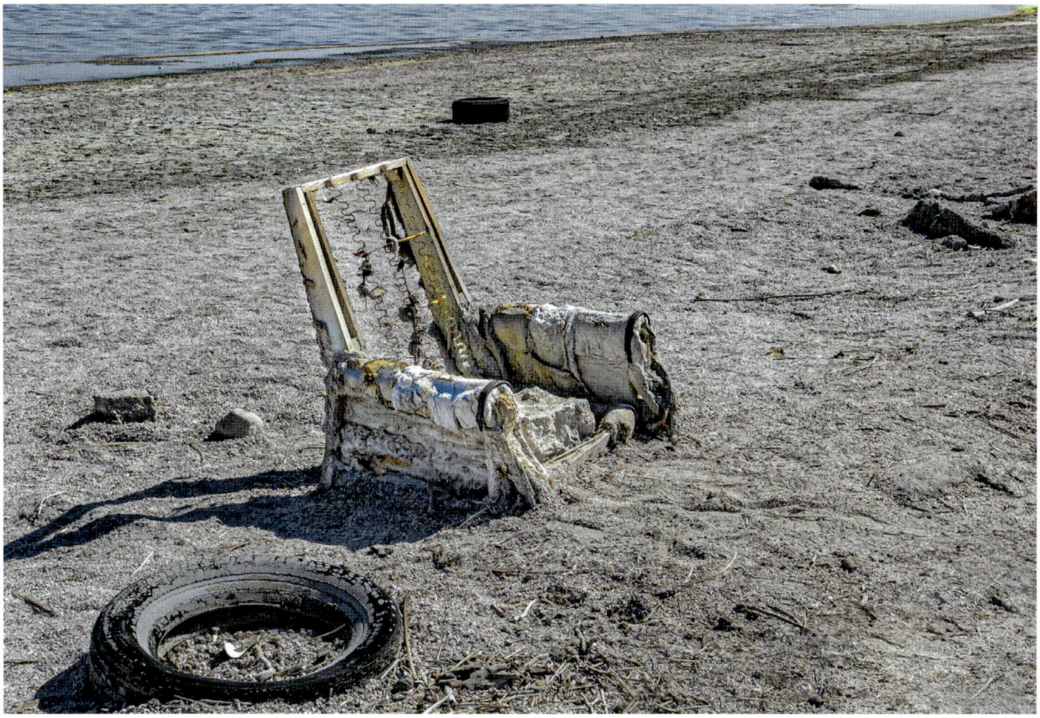

A CAST-OFF CHAIR ON DESERT SHORES BEACH: The Salton Sea is seated on the San Andreas Fault and spans Riverside and Imperial Counties.

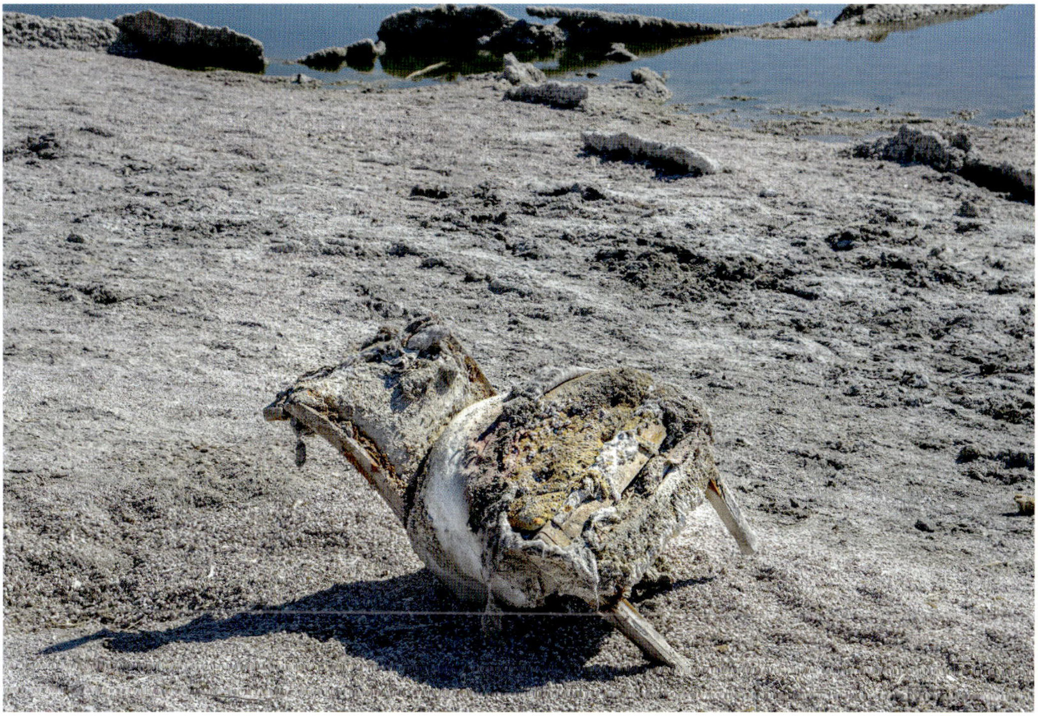

DESERT SHORES CHAIR: 10,000 years ago, the Salton Sea was a dry lake bed known as the Salton Sink.

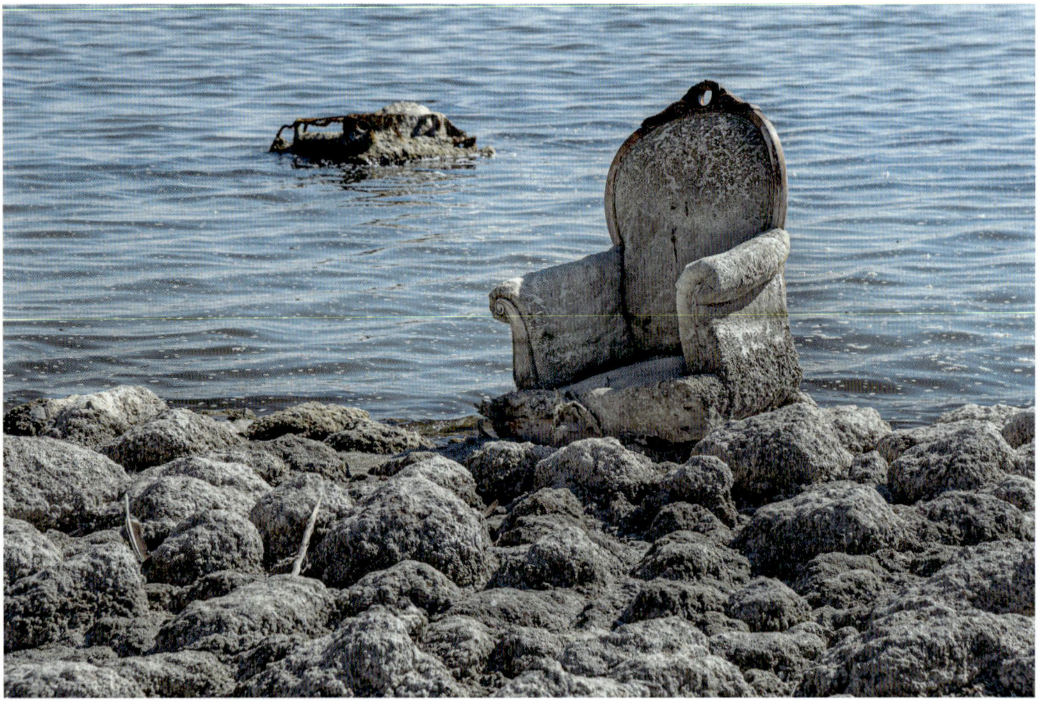

NEPTUNE'S CHAIR ON DESERT SHORES: After the Colorado River breach in 1905, the Salton Sea was a freshwater lake, but by the 1960s, salinity levels sharply rose higher than the Pacific Ocean.

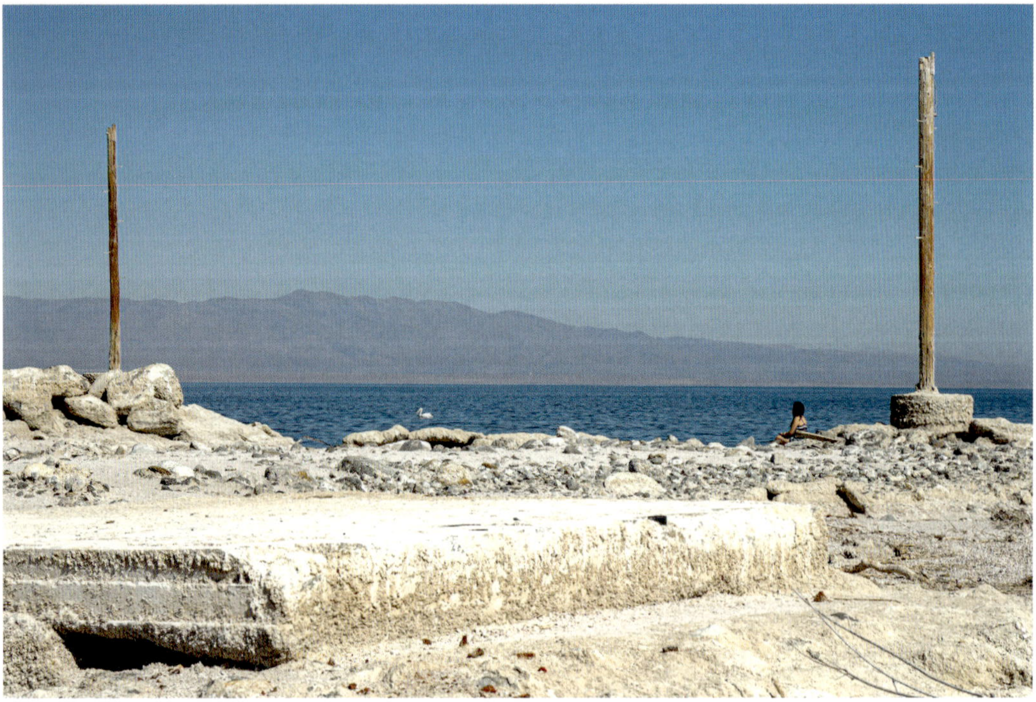

DESERT SHORES: The community of Desert Shores holds a few businesses, including a bar, a restaurant, and bodega-like grocery store.

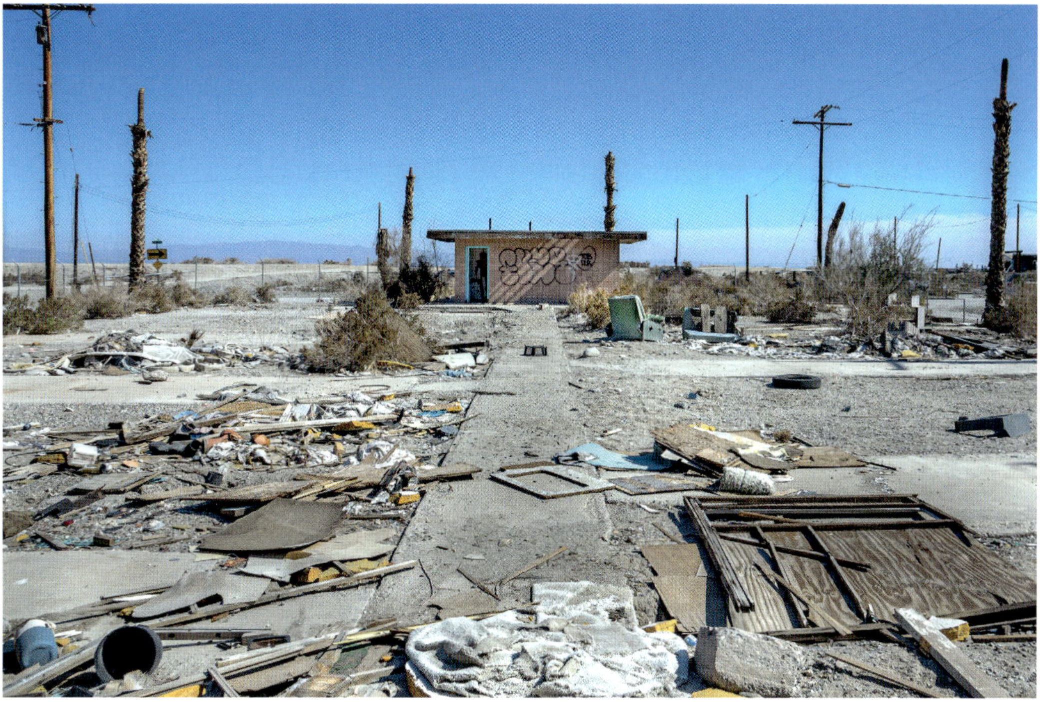

SALTON CITY BEACH: Although it is the largest "city" development on the Sea shoreline, most of Salton City's roads are undeveloped or deteriorating. Likewise, the marina, abandoned homes, and bits of former docks are crumbling monuments to better times.

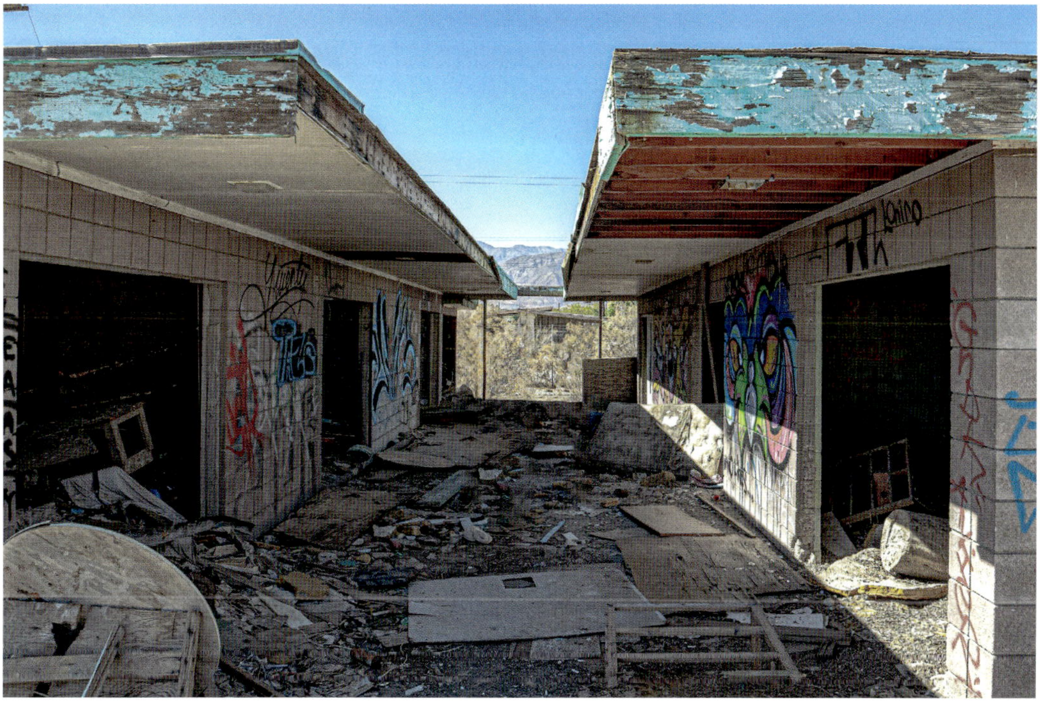

ABANDONED HOUSING: The coastal town of Salton City is in ruins.

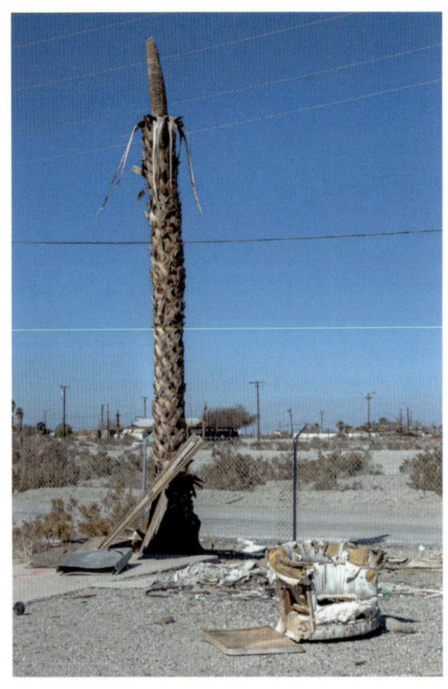

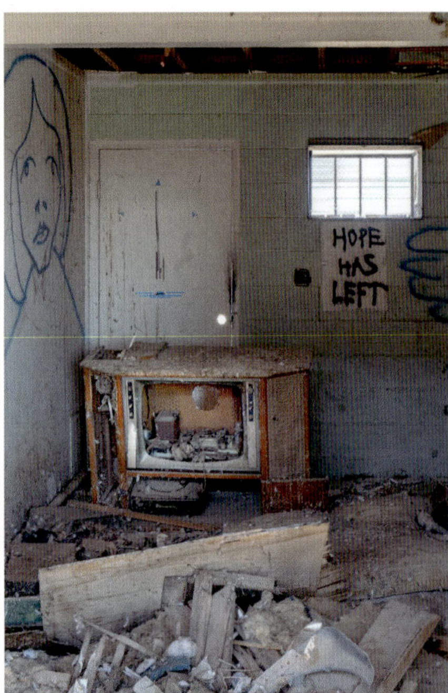

◀ **SALTON CITY BEACH:** Salton Sea region residents face constant exposure to dangerous fine airborne chemical dust from the evaporating Sea.

▶ **REMAINS:** Salton City Beach was once a popular speedboat destination. The Sea's high salinity increased boat buoyancy, and because the area is at 200 feet below sea level, the barometric pressure increased speedboat performance.

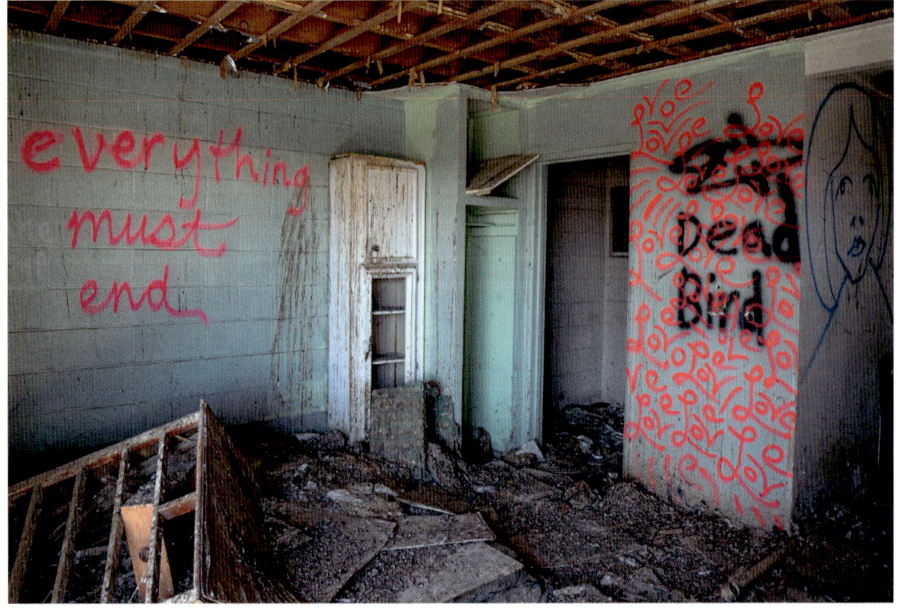

EVERYTHING MUST END – SALTON CITY: Early Salton City developers wanted to replicate the success of the nearby desert resort town, Palm Springs.

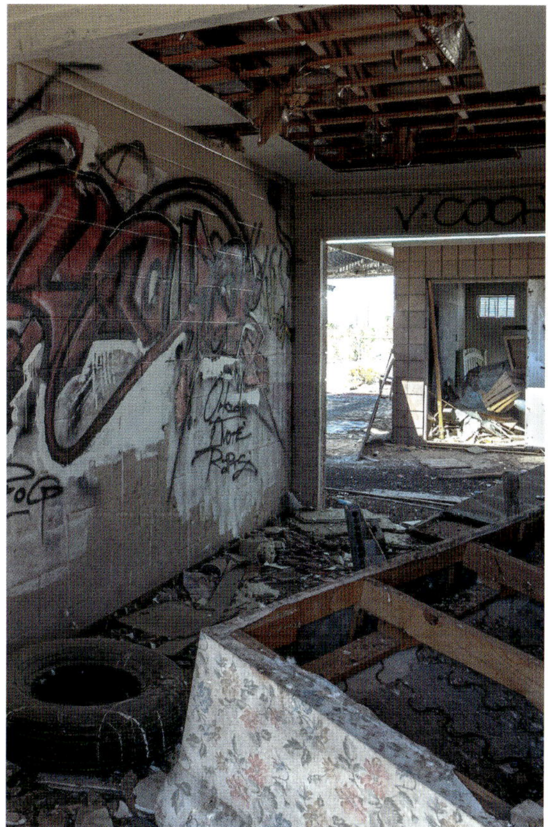

▲ **ABANDONED HOUSING:** After releasing fish into the Sea, by the late 1950s, the Salton Sea was a popular fishing destination and California's most productive fishery.

▼ **SALTON CITY BUSINESS REMAINS:** President Eisenhower golfed in the Salton Sea Region, and the Beach Boys, Frank Sinatra, and Jerry Lewis were frequent Sea region entertainers.

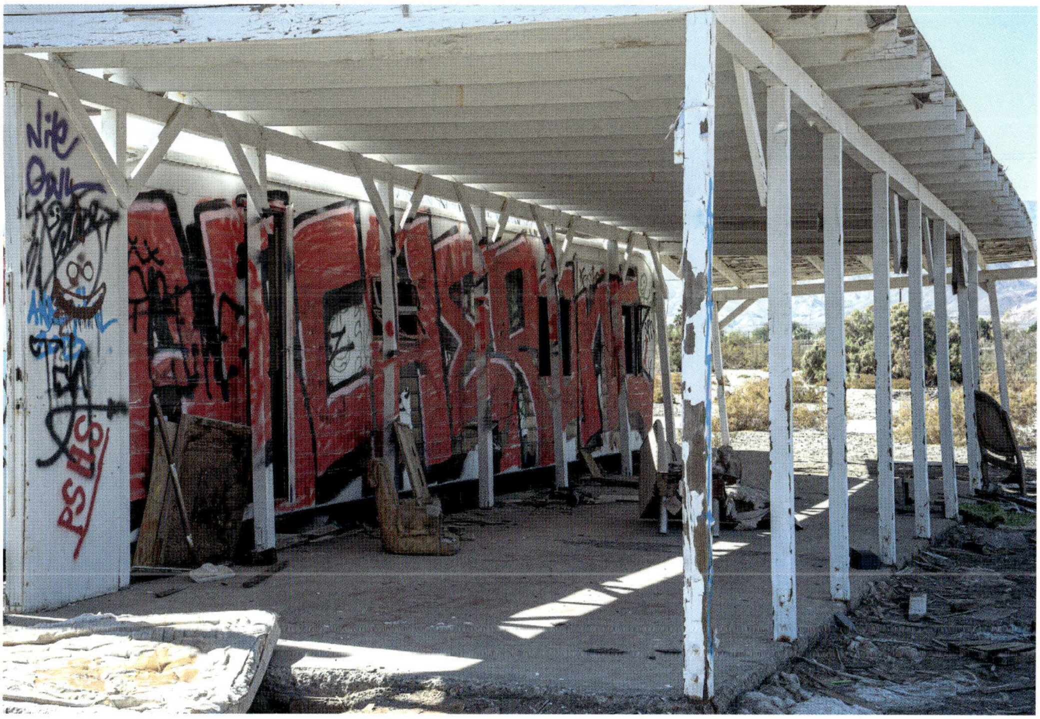

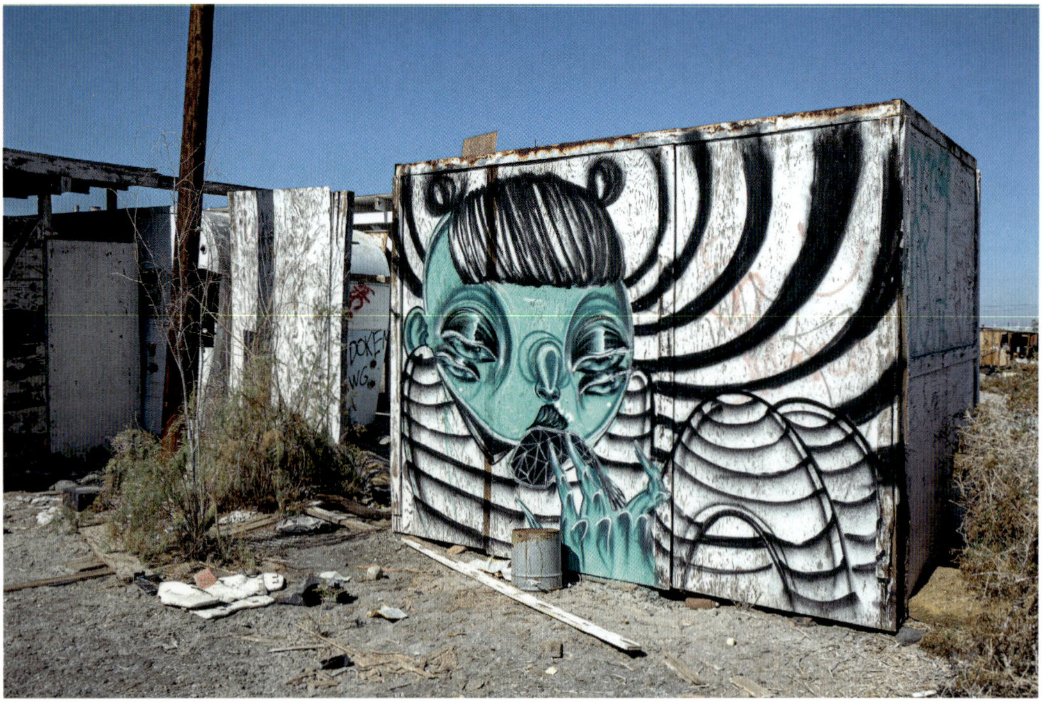

SALTON CITY RUINS: With the sea evaporating rapidly, a rising flooding sea level is no longer a concern.

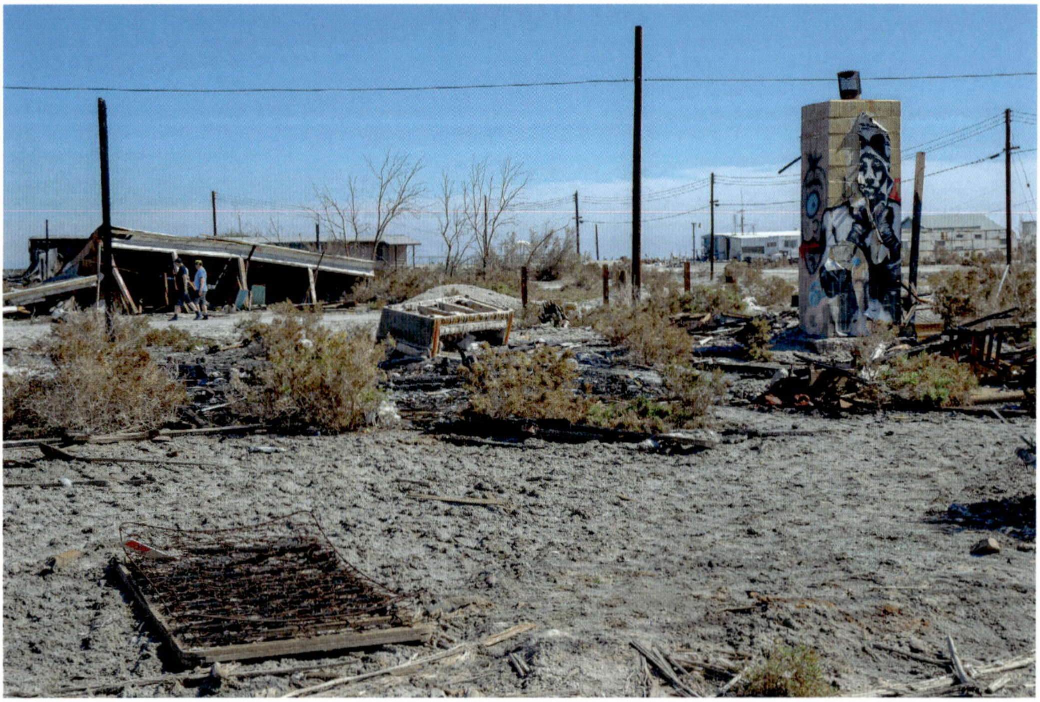

SALTON CITY VESTIGES: In 2018, a water transfer agreement with San Diego resulted in 40 percent less water flowing into the Salton Sea, thus prompting more evaporation and a greater release of pollutants into the air from the drying Sea bed.

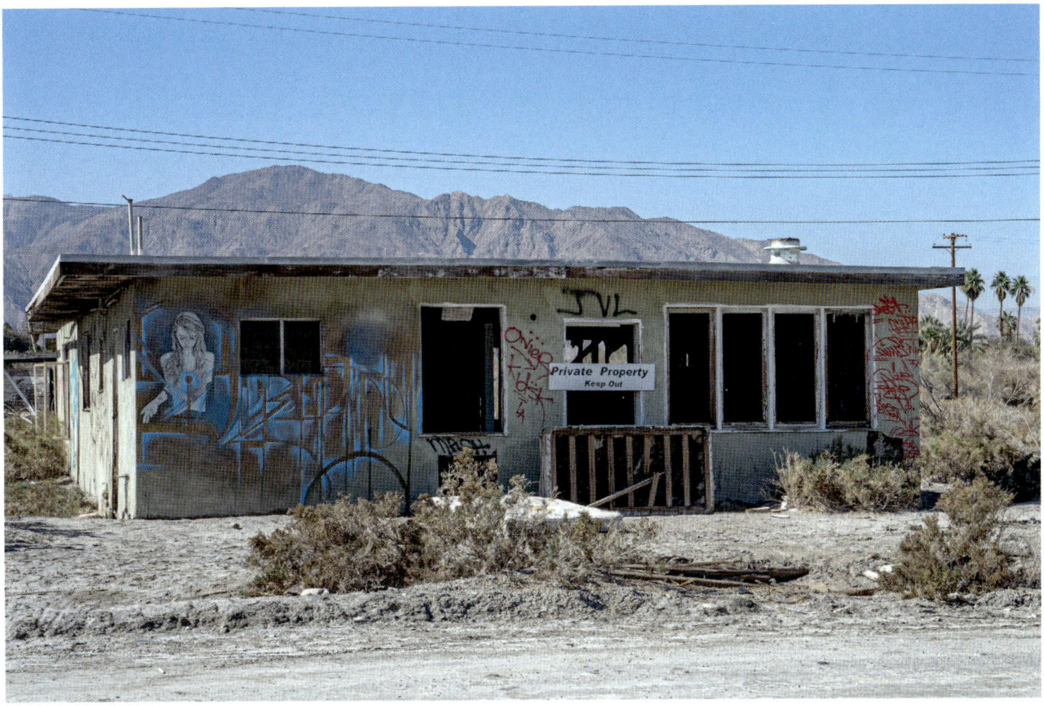

RUINS: Salton City was established in 1958 and realized development into the 1960s courtesy of M. Penn Phillips and the Holly Corporation.

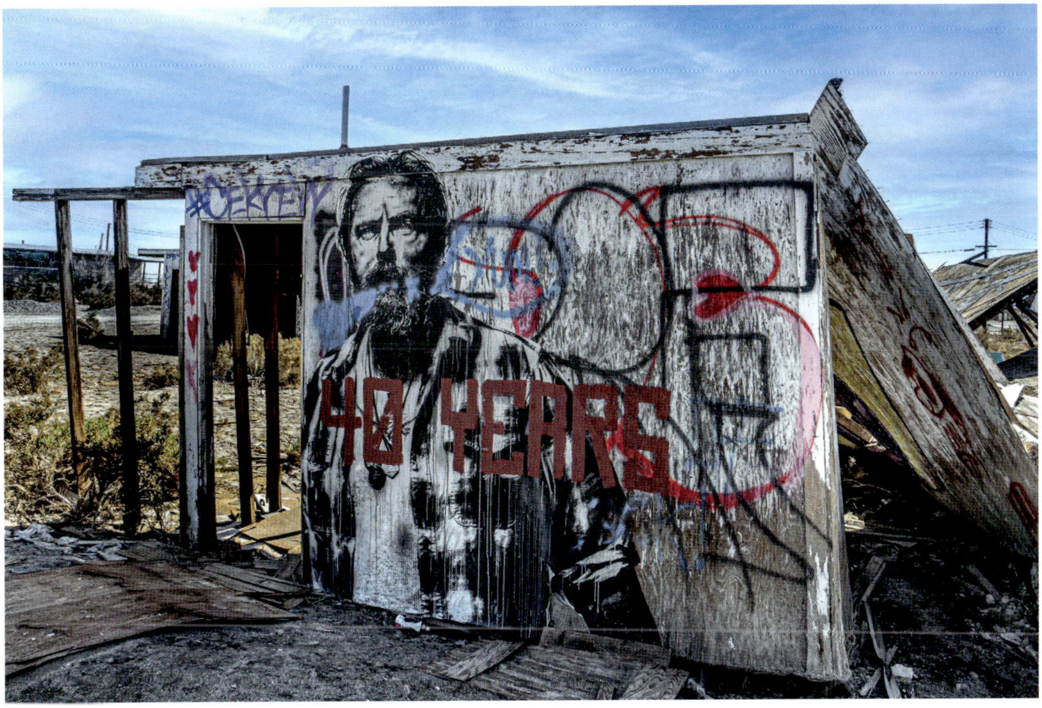

SALTON CITY DETRITUS: The salt-filled air and continuous sunlight accelerate the erosion of derelict structures and debris that surround the Sea.

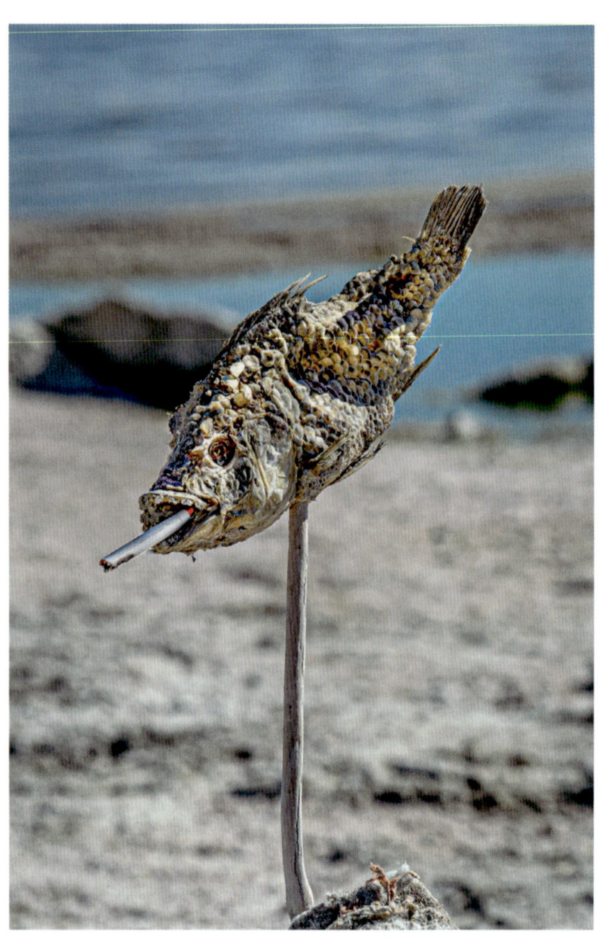

▲ **SMOKING KILLS:** Environmentalists warn that as the Salton Sea continues to evaporate, more and more toxic dust will be carried by heavy winds and into distant locales, with compounding health issues.

▼ **SALTON CITY GHOST BEACH:** Salton Sea's beachfront property is relatively inexpensive, and the coastline is constantly receding.

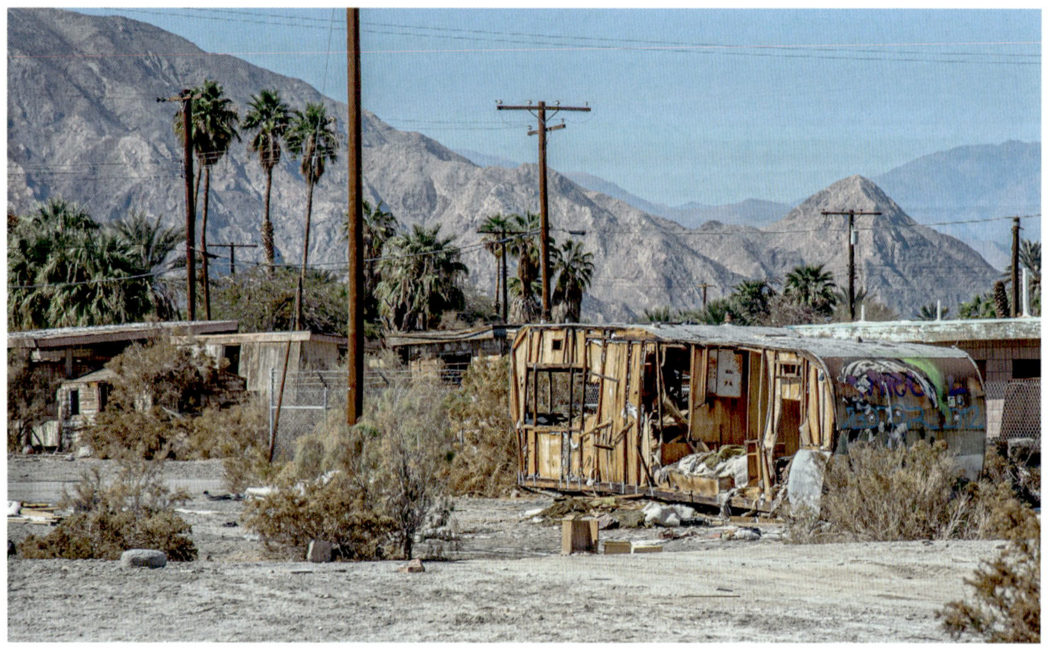

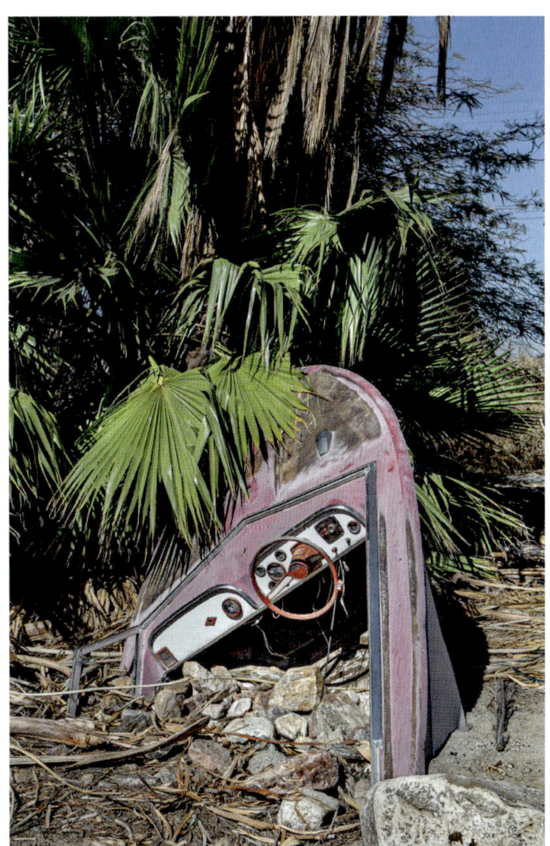

▲ **ABANDONED BOAT:** The Salton Sea basin is 8,360 square miles. The Salton Sea is California's largest lake.

▼ **SHUTTERED SANS SOUCI CLUB:** *Sans Souci* is French for "no worries."

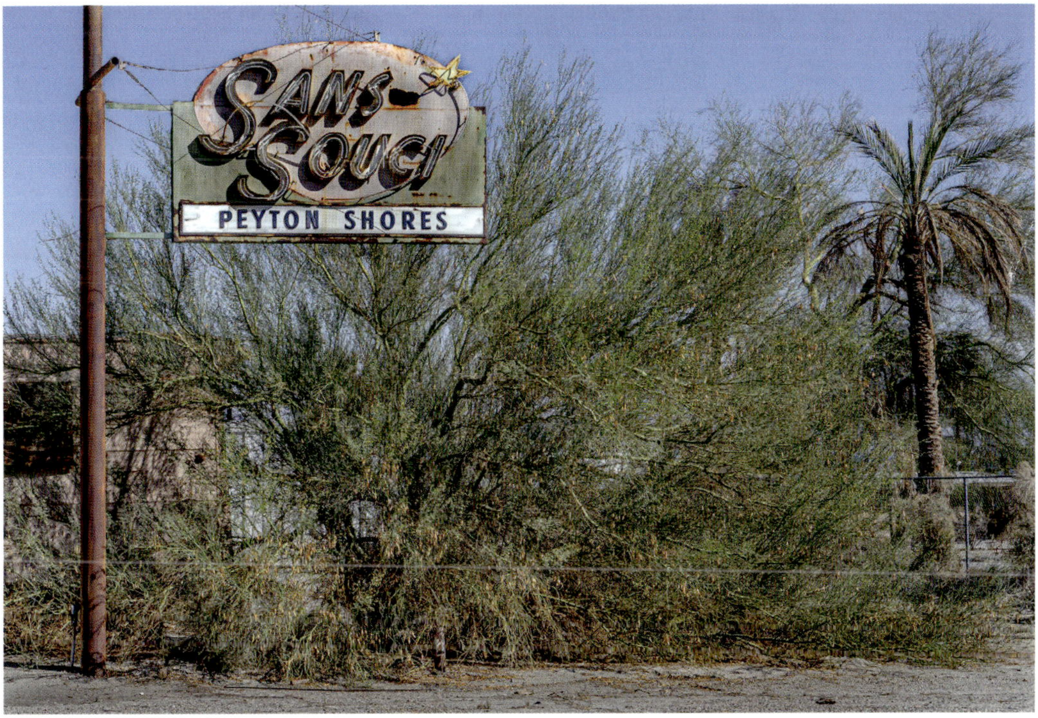

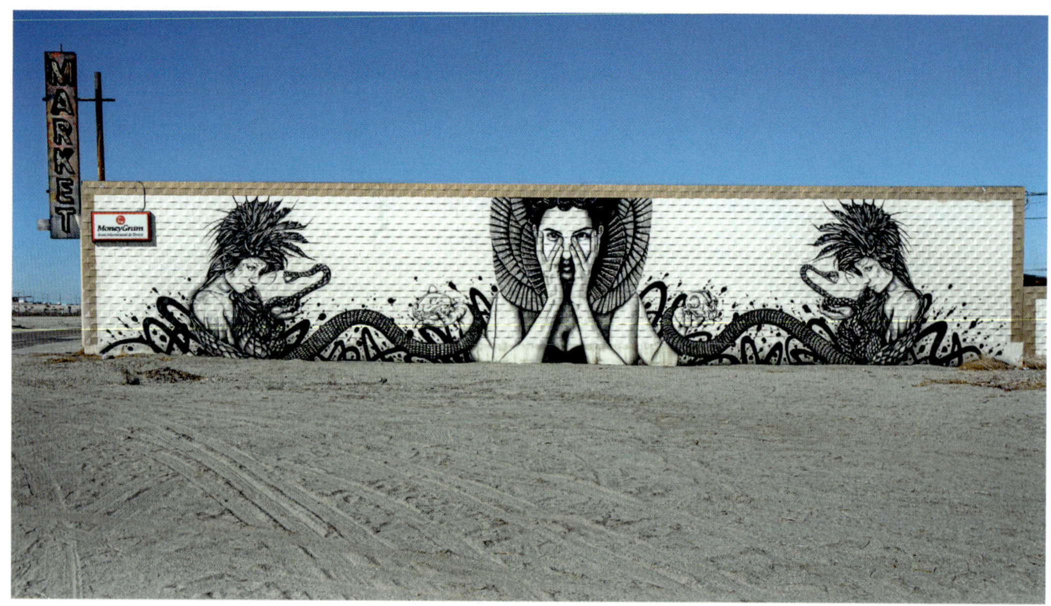

DESERT SHORES MARKET: The street art on a west shores market wall, by artists Fin DAC and Angelina Christina, collectively known as the "Bad Ass Chicks," is called, Shesha Sand Storm.

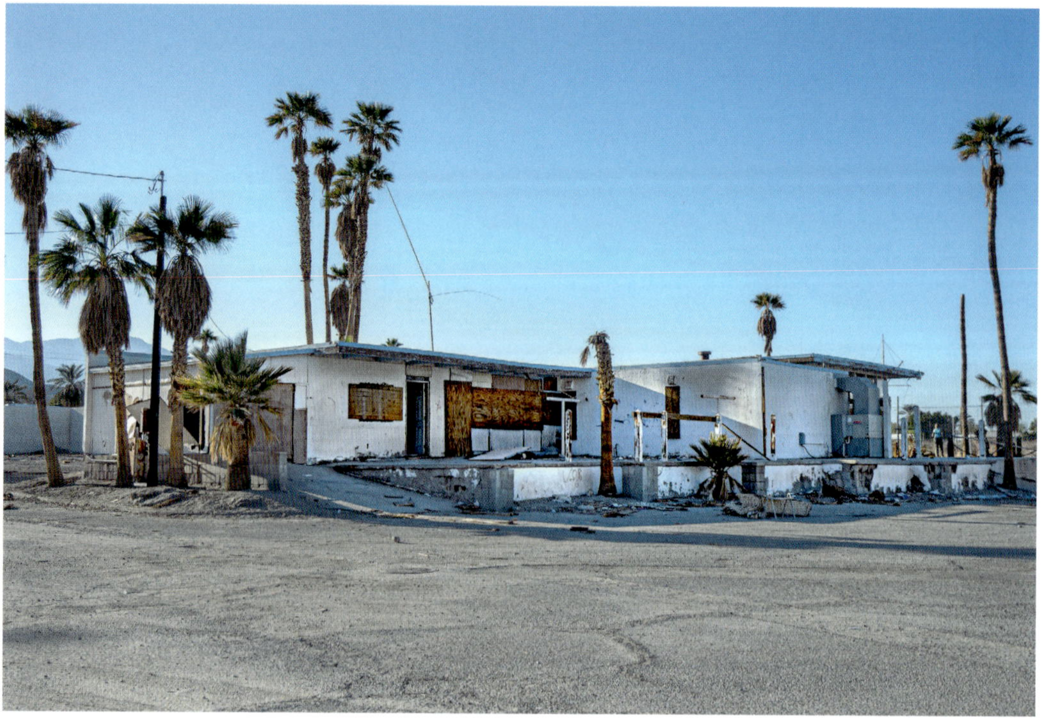

FORMER MARINA MOBILE ESTATES CLUB: This former Desert Shores beach club was recently demolished.

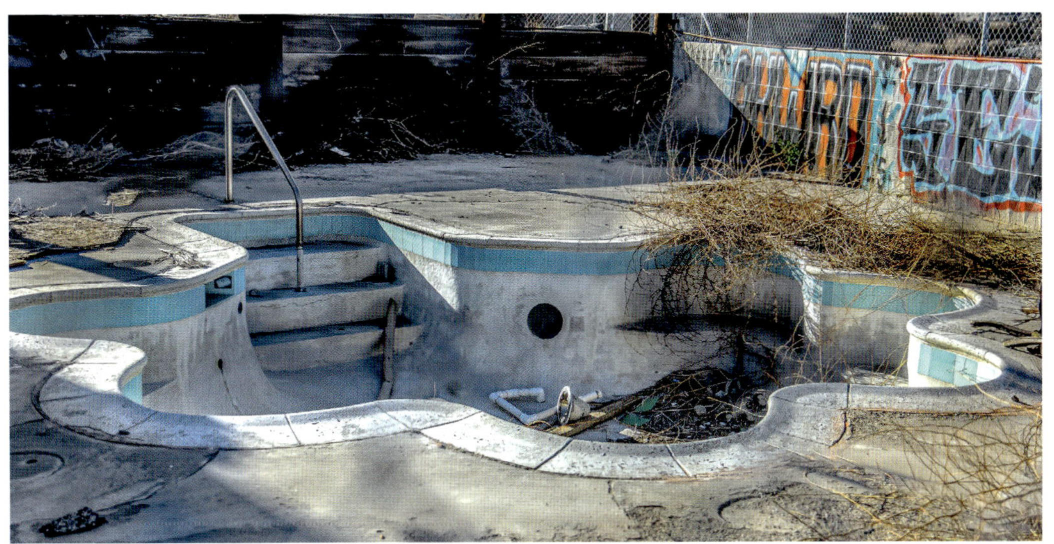

SPA POOL OF FORMER MARINA MOBILE ESTATES CLUB: The spa pool of a community club house is framed by graffiti and desolation.

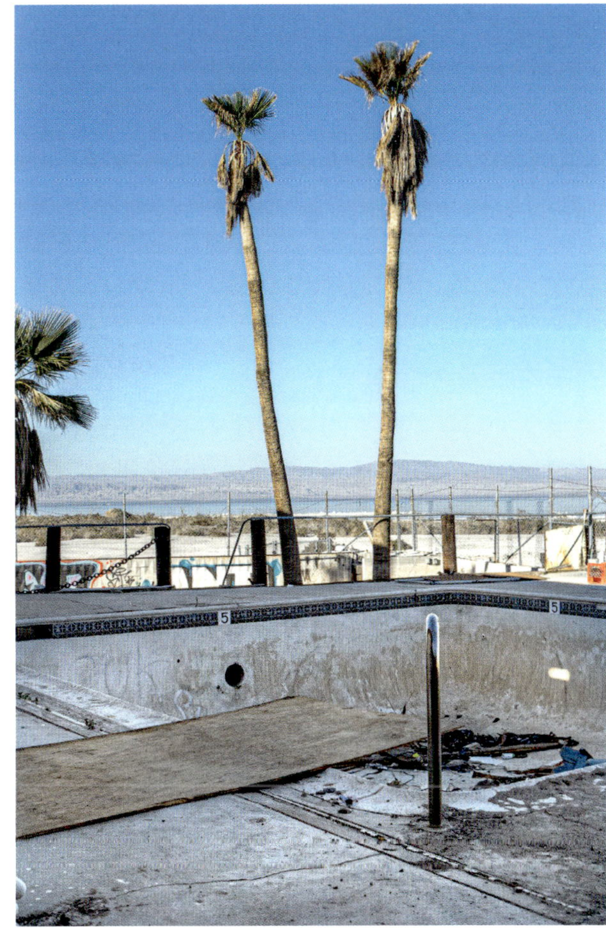

POOL OF FORMER MARINA MOBILE ESTATES CLUB: The larger in-ground pool of a community beach club revealed lovely Desert Shores beach and sea views.

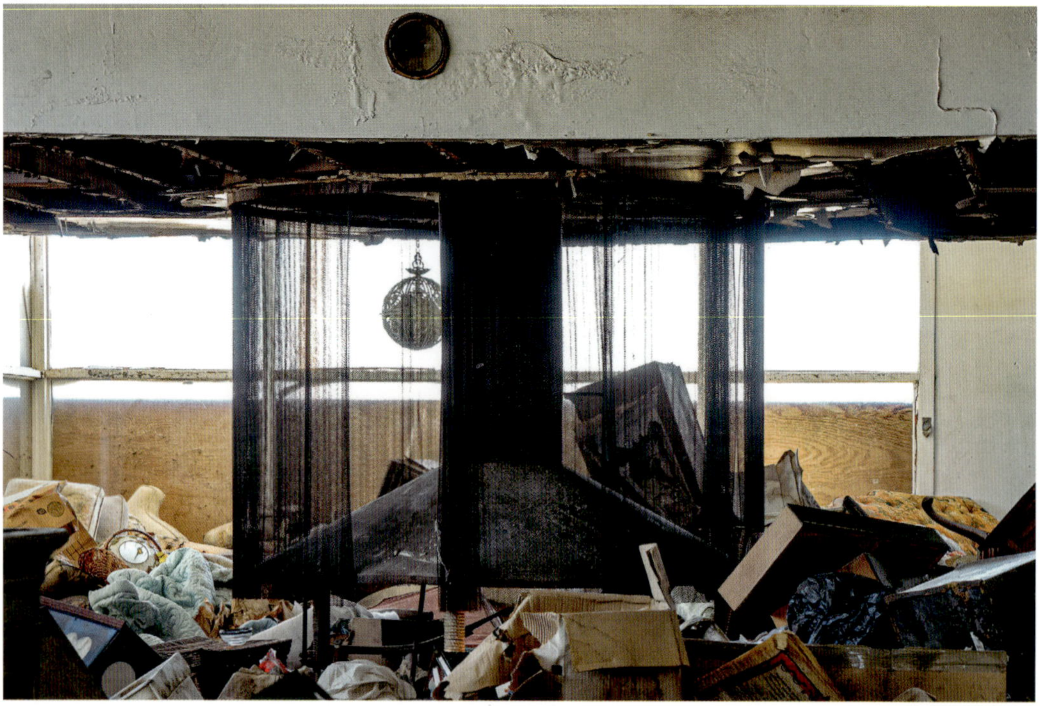

MARINA MOBILE ESTATES CLUB 360 DEGREE FIREPLACE: The interior of the abandoned club was stuffed with so much debris that it obscured the beautiful window views and lovely floorplan its members once enjoyed.

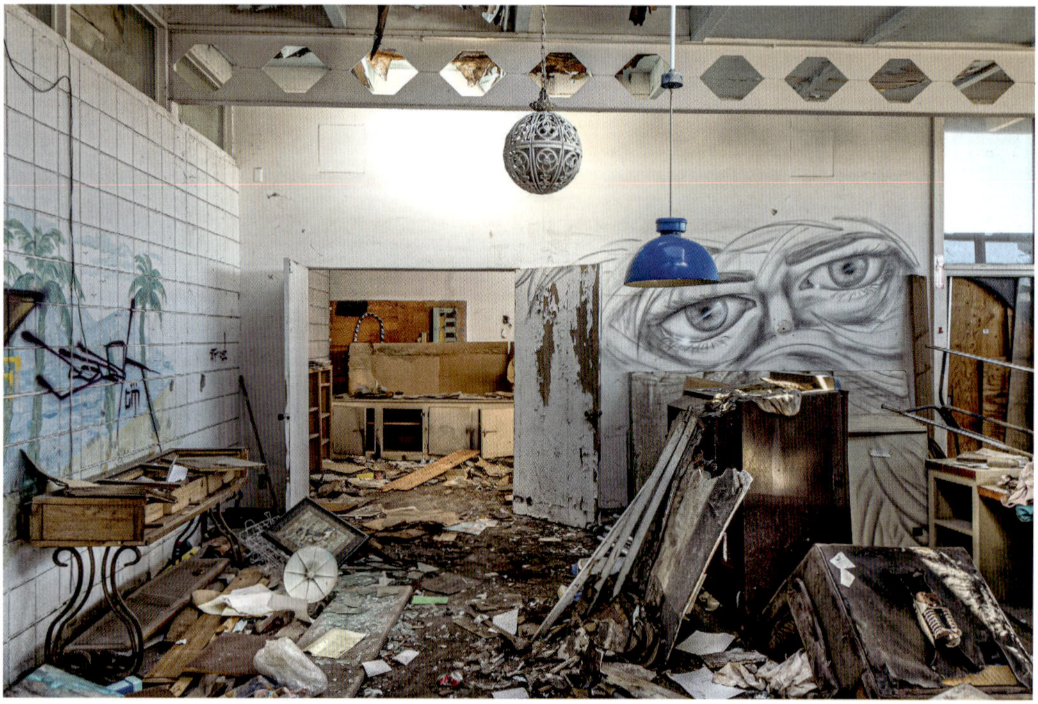

MARINA MOBILE ESTATES CLUB: The club was wide open and allowed vandals to enter and ransack the contents inside as well as provide several canvases for graffitists.

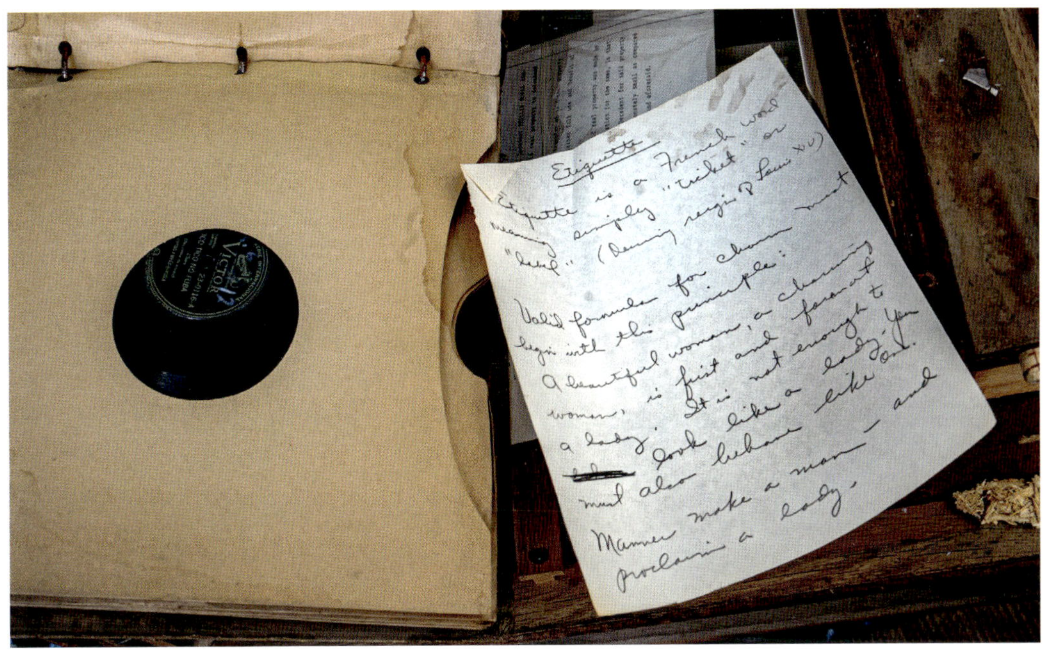

CLUB ARTIFACTS: Antique artifacts, such as these seventy-eight records, were found inside. The words on the note revealed: "Etiquette is a French word meaning simply 'ticket' or 'label' (During reign of Louis XIV). Valid formula for charm must begin with the principle: a beautiful woman, a charming woman, is first and foremost a lady. It is not enough to look like a lady. You must also behave like one. Manners make a man—and proclaim a lady."

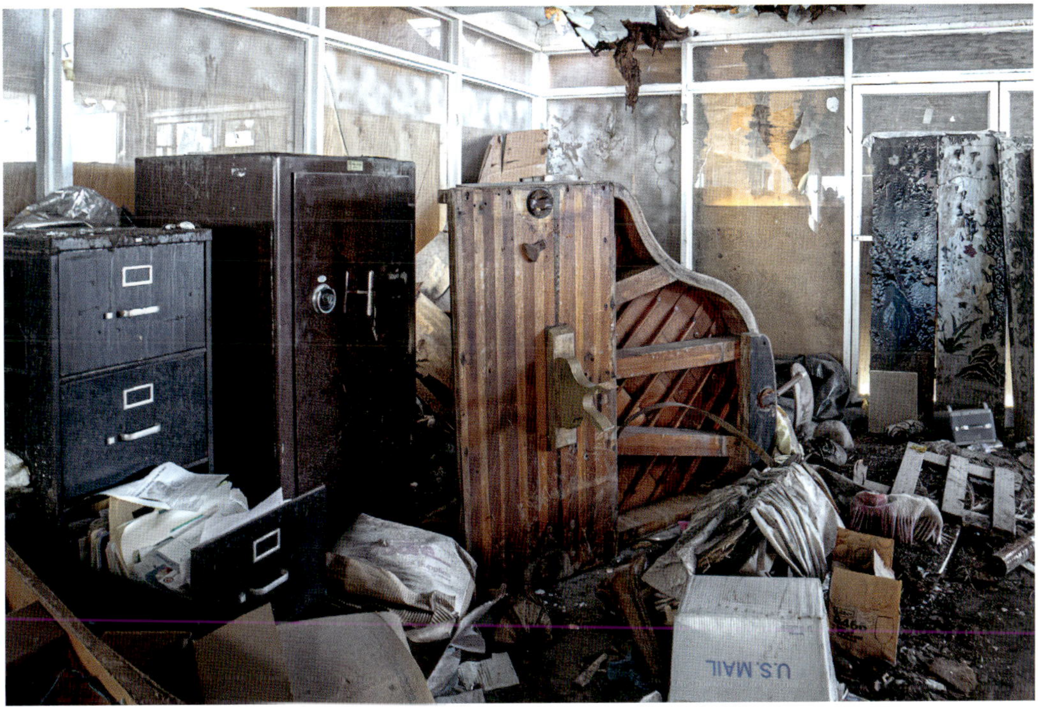

CLUB OFFICE: A grand piano on its side shared space with the former Marina Mobile Estates Club office.

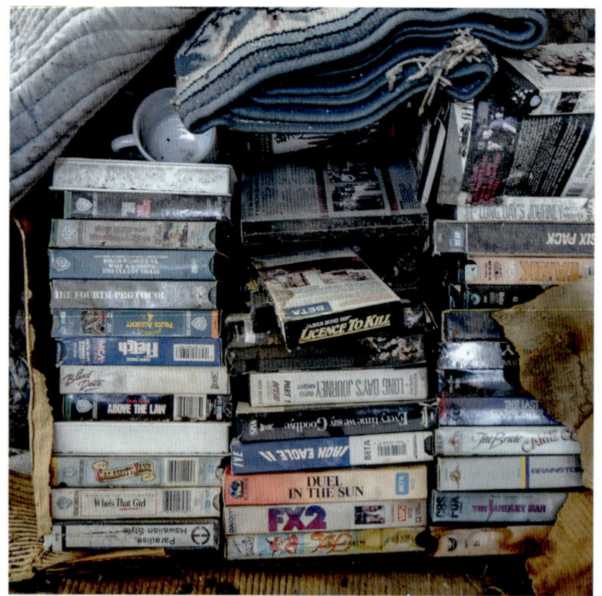

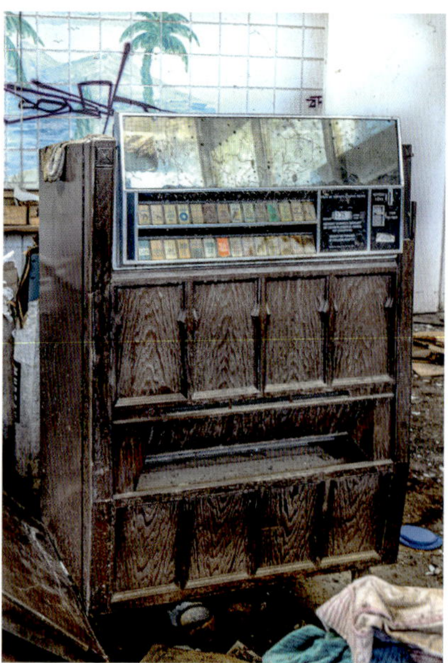

◄ **CLUB RELICS:** Betamax and VHS tapes of old movies were stacked in a corner. The amount of debris inside the club was overwhelming.

► **CLUB CIGARETTE MACHINE:** A vintage cigarette machine was once a Marina Mobile Estates Club fixture. Cigarette vending machines were declared illegal in the U.S. on June 22, 2010, except in establishments restricting all to eighteen years and older.

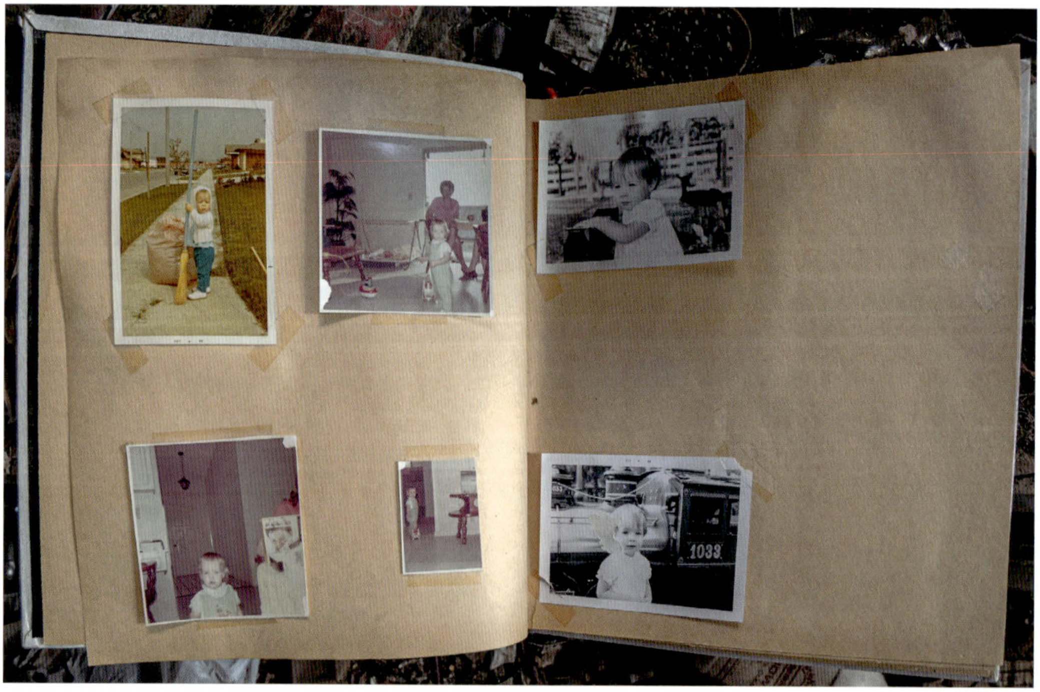

CLUB MEMENTOS: Several family photo albums amid the artifacts. Did no family members want to preserve these memories?

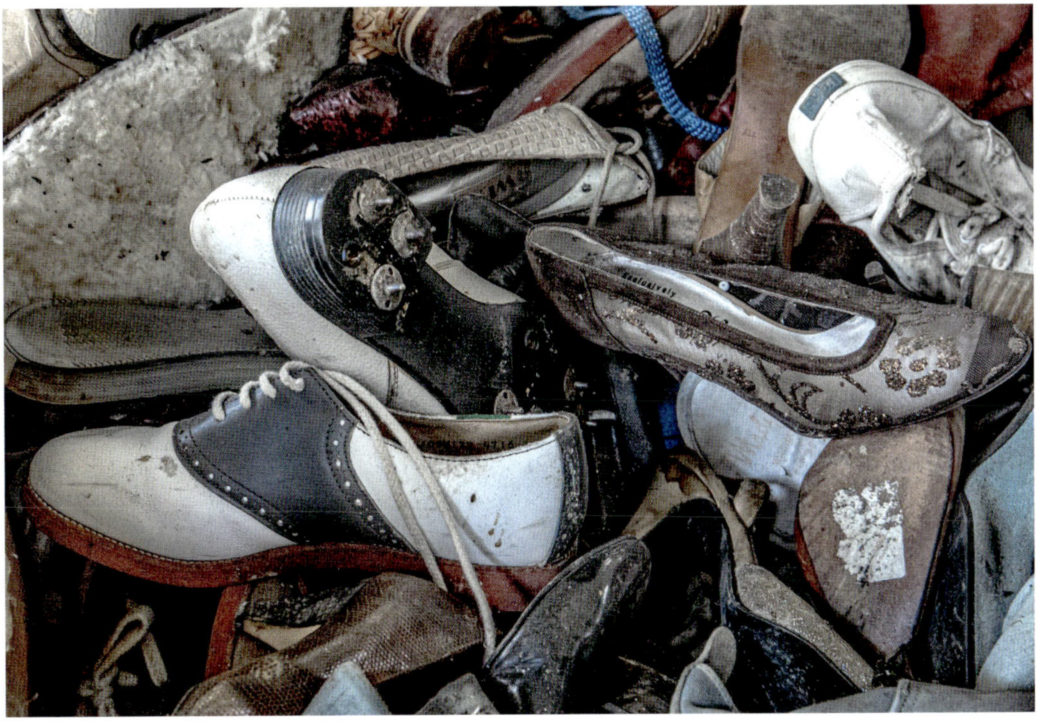

▲ **SHOES:** An odd collection of shoes was inside the Marina Mobile Estates Club. I suspect this site was a dumping ground for the community as much of the interior content did not fit the structure's original recreational purpose.

▼ **DESERT SHORES FIRE STATION:** Although not abandoned, the Desert Shores Fire Station revealed tattered U.S. and California flags, and to my urbex eye, an appropriate look for the flavor of the environment.

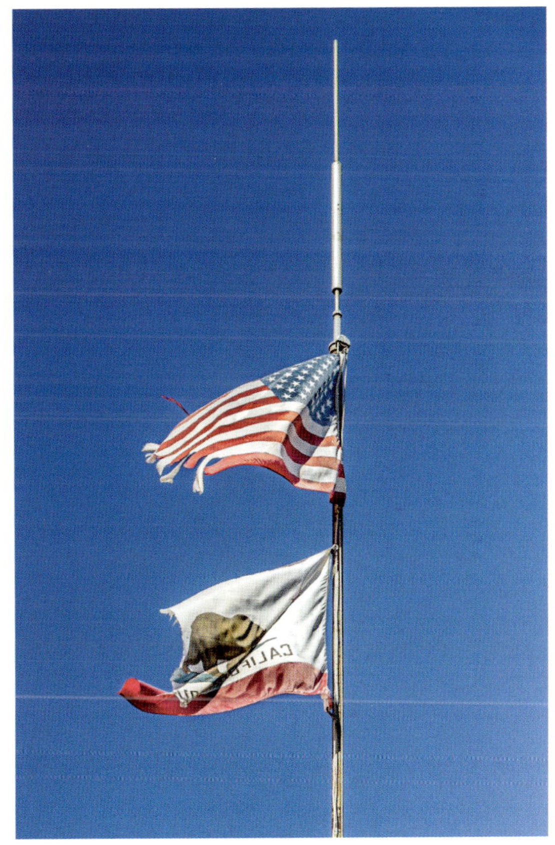

3

THE COLORFUL UNABANDONED LEGACY OF SAVING ONE'S SOUL

Ramping up Salton Sea's quirkiness factor are a few attractions and communities on the east side—Salvation Mountain, Slab City, and the Slab's sub-community of East Jesus. While all these unusual roadside finds are adjacent to each other, they deserve individual chapters, but I will start with the colorful Salvation Mountain ("Mountain"). Salvation Mountain is not abandoned, and its creator, Leonard Knight (1931-2014), left such a vivid mark on the landscape that his art, message, and legacy live. Still, the permanence of Salvation Mountain is always in jeopardy, and could one day be installed within the forsaken dossier. First impressions of Salvation Mountain have one pondering if the site is charming, fabulous, or tacky. Maybe it is all three rolled into one enchanting peculiarity. Charming because once you gaze at the vibrant hand-painted Mountain, you want to learn more about it, and you have the compulsion to experience its large footprint of dizzying color. It is fabulous because the site's appearance makes me nostalgic for the psychedelic sixties. It is tacky, too, but in an innocuous way. The creation of Salvation Mountain's art is an ongoing creative process and a testament to Knight's influence and inspiration.

The history of Salvation Mountain reveals one man's gallant long-term homage to God. No one misses the behemoth "God is Love" painted at the Mountain peak. A closer examination of the expansive "art piece" reveals additional scripture such as the Lord's Prayer, John 3:16, and the Sinner's Prayer. Adornments such as flowers, trees, waterfalls, suns, birds, and other chromatic delights complement the sacred text. Salvation Mountain is 50-feet high and constructed with local adobe clay bricks, tires, windowpanes, metal pieces, and countless gallons of donated paint.

A sign requesting donated paint greets all who enter—a paint drive instead of the usual food drive. Recycling formed a dynamic artful Mountain. Courtesy of Leonard Knight, the message of love appears in every corner, crevice, inside, and outside of Salvation Mountain. One can climb the Mountain to the peak by way of a yellow brick road, even though, technically, Salvation Mountain is not a mountain. Only three stories to the summit, the apex provides an expansive view of the desert and surrounding areas, including its neighbor, Slab City. One can walk the Mountain's interior museum caverns, too.

Leonard Knight was born in Burlington, Vermont, on November 1, 1931. Knight, a victim of school bullying because of his stutter, dropped out of school in the tenth grade. Knight served in the Korean War but had difficulty establishing roots after his army discharge. Then, at thirty-six, Knight had a religious epiphany while sitting in his van. Knight claimed a passion for God suddenly overtook his soul and prompted his immediate and repeated recitations of the Sinner's Prayer. Knight asserted his life changed for the better, and thus, vowed to go forth and spread God's love. Shortly after his spiritual awakening, Knight relocated to Nebraska to fulfill his pledge. Still, after ten years of unsuccessful attempts to construct a hot air balloon as his spiritual marketing tool, Knight trekked to California's desert. After settling in California, Knight commenced with the assembly of Salvation Mountain as his tribute to God. Possessing only a bucket, a shovel, and a bag of cement, Knight inaugurated his divine project and continued to add more cement, sand, debris, and refuse from a nearby dump. The final stage clothed the Mountain in colorful paint, scripture, and themes of love. After four years, though, Salvation Mountain collapsed, but Knight was not deterred and launched another mountain fabrication project possessing permanence for posterity.

In 1989, Knight launched the second Salvation Mountain project but now incorporated construction with traditional Navajo adobe clay bricks and straw. More than thirty years later, Salvation Mountain still stands along with its many layers of colorful paint. The Mountain's interior is the museum, and its caverns hold trees, walkways, and vivid patterns. A small shrine rests inside, too, with devout pilgrims from all over the world signing the guest register and leaving trinkets and personal tokens as offerings of their faith.

While Knight passed away in 2014, his message still resonates with the many Salvation Mountain volunteers and visitors. Knight was adamant about dispatching his voice to the world in a universal and straightforward Christian message—God is all about love, accept the way of Jesus, and atone for any sinful ways. Knight believed his happy art and message would reverberate to all, Christians and non-Christians alike.

Salvation Mountain continues to face challenges and more so with the passing of Knight. The Imperial Valley's harsh summers, air pollution, and strong winds inflict a toll on all fabricated surfaces. Currently, the Mountain is cared for under the auspices of Salvation Mountain, Inc.—a non-profit organization. Nevertheless, Knight's vision is always in peril because of environmental threats and the political and public pressures to shutter the unusual attraction. Knight's legacy is revered because of the efforts of Salvation Mountain's voluntary preservation soldiers to perpetuate Knight's unabandoned gift for the masses. In an area owning so much ecological destruction and sadness and devoid of so much color, it would be doleful to lose such a dazzling and optimistic landmark—any cognizance of sanguinity, especially Knight's clay heirloom, should be embraced, and not abandoned, within this wounded land.

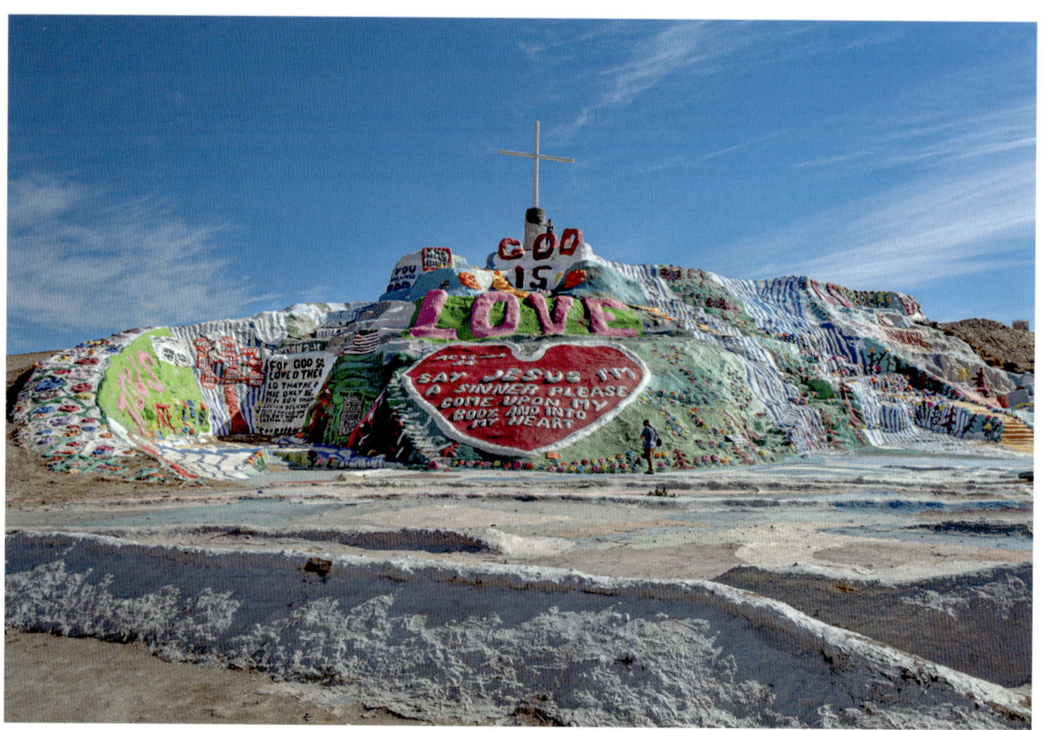

SALVATION MOUNTAIN: Salvation Mountain was the spiritual inspiration and creation of Leonard Knight (1931-2014).

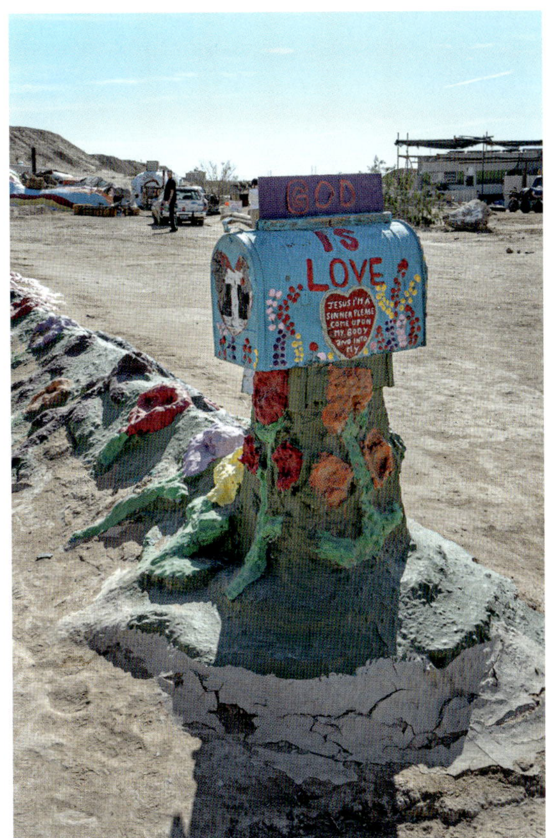

▲ **THE MOUNTAIN MAILBOX:** The theme of love is omnipresent at Salvation Mountain.

▼ **LEONARD KNIGHT'S QUARTERS:** At thirty-six, Knight experienced a sudden passion for God. Initially, Knight unsuccessfully attempted to spread the word of God via a hot air balloon.

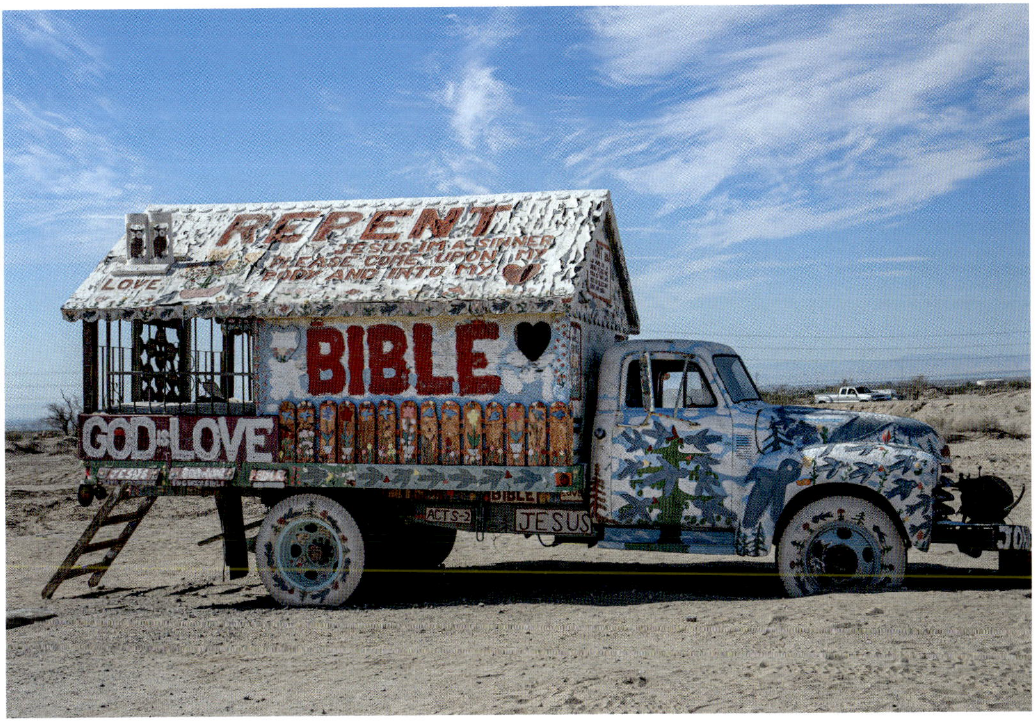

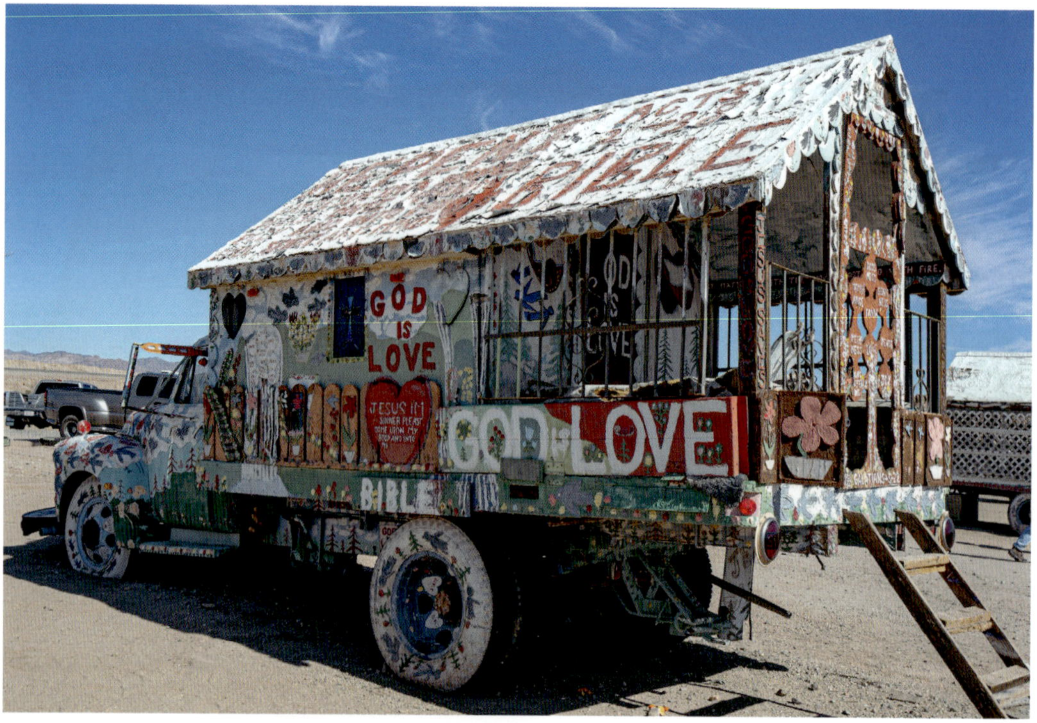

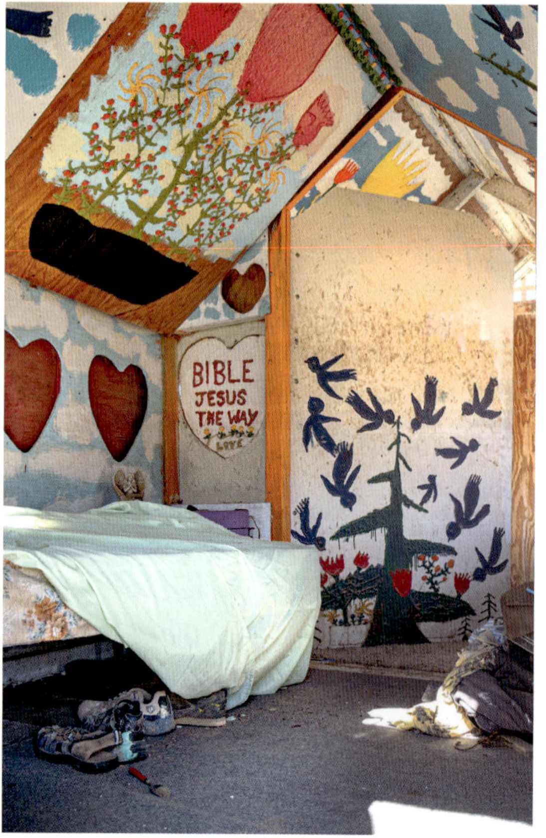

▲ **LEONARD KNIGHT'S QUARTERS:** In a final attempt to spread his message, Knight moved to southern California and started to erect a monument in Niland, near Slab Cityul—ultimately Salvation Mountain.

▼ **INTERIOR OF LEONARD KNIGHT'S QUARTERS:** Knight's vision of Salvation Mountain formed with a bucket, shovel, and a bag of cement.

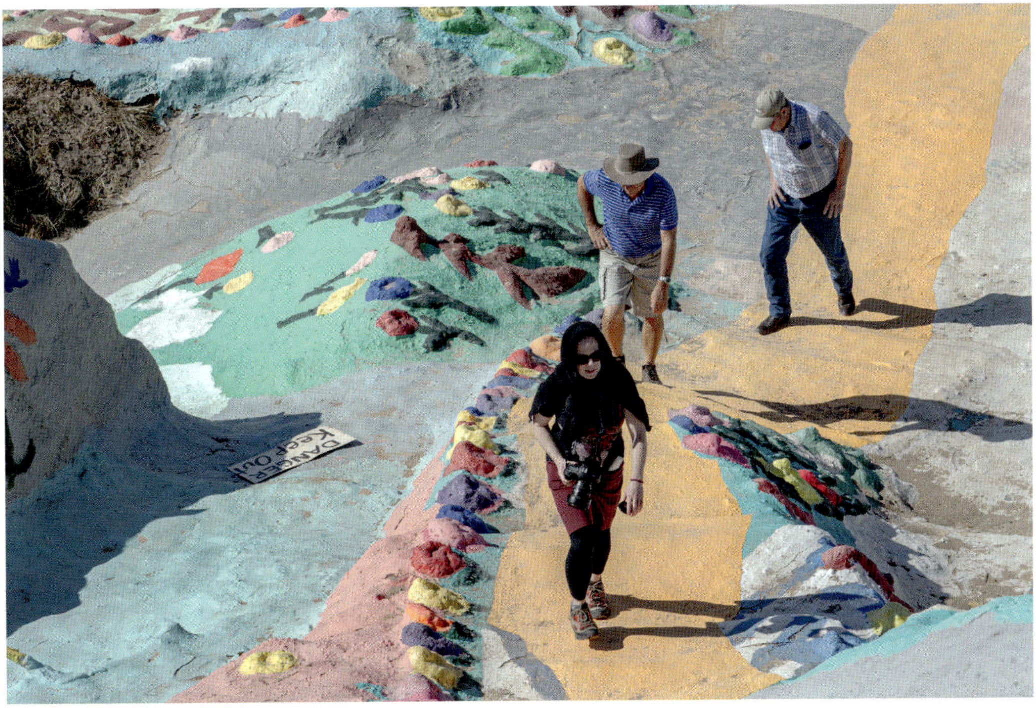

HIKING THE YELLOW BRICK ROAD TO THE APEX: Salvation Mountain collapsed into dust after four years, but Knight resumed construction and built a more secure monument.

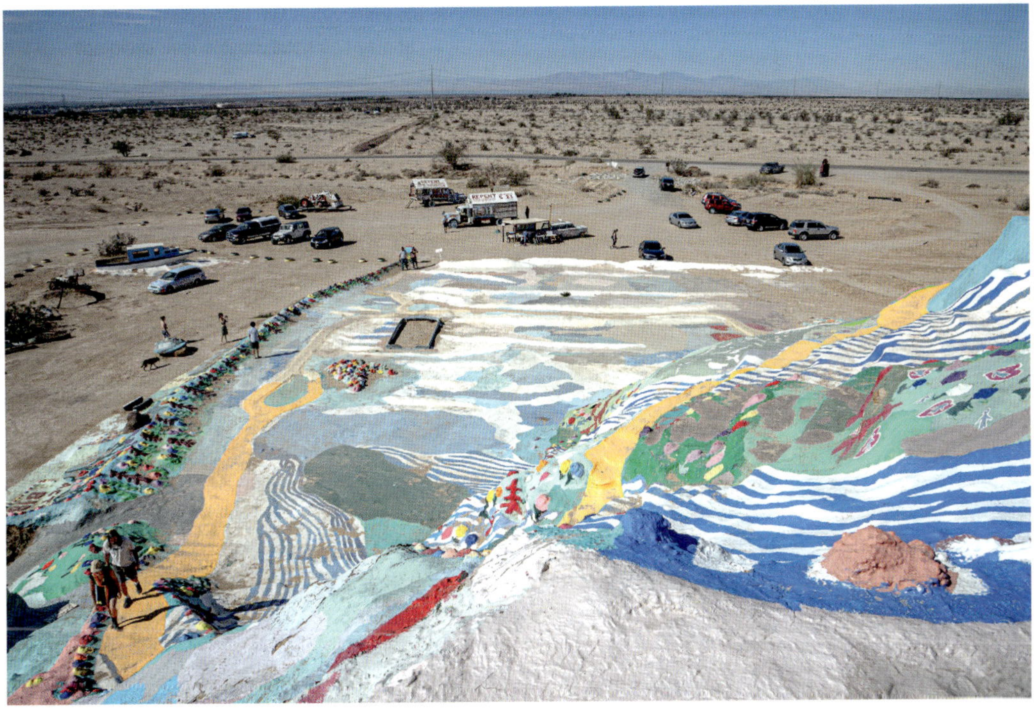

MOUNTAINTOP OVERLOOK: The second Salvation Mountain was built with adobe clay and straw and allowed for stability and permanence.

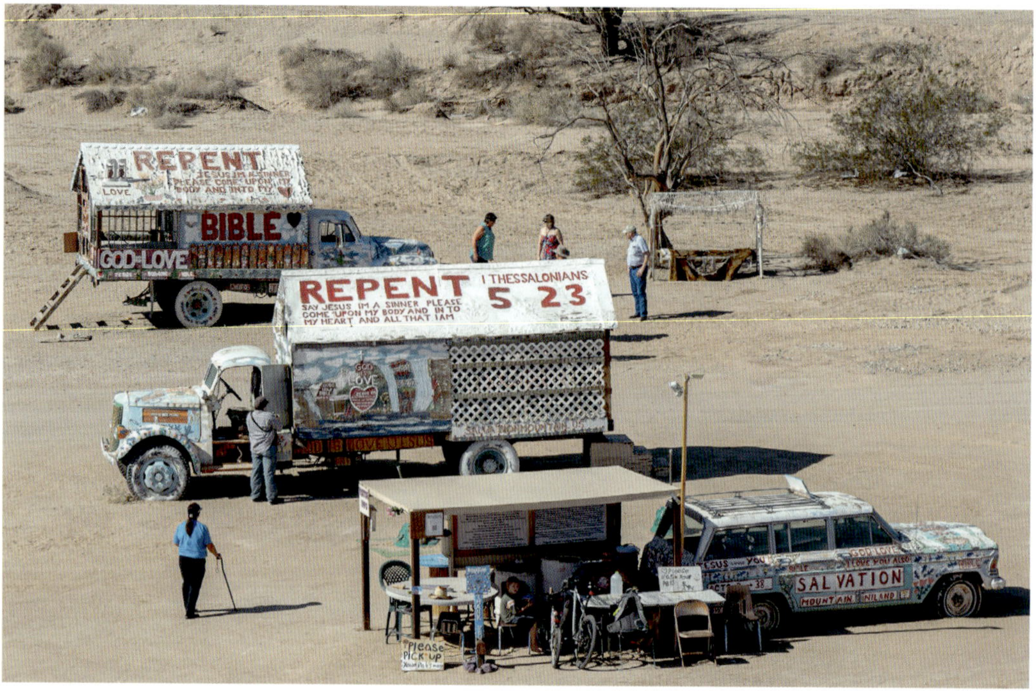

VIEW FROM THE TOP: Salvation Mountain is approximately three stories tall.

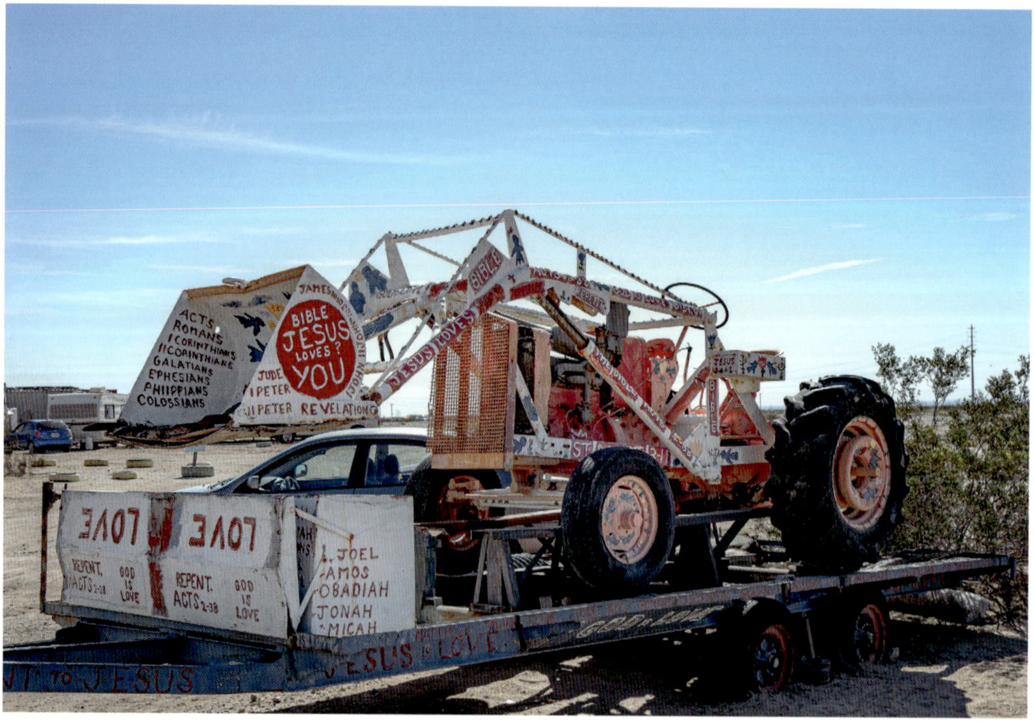

CONSTRUCTION EQUIPMENT: The mountain's earth mover is also adorned with scripture and love messages.

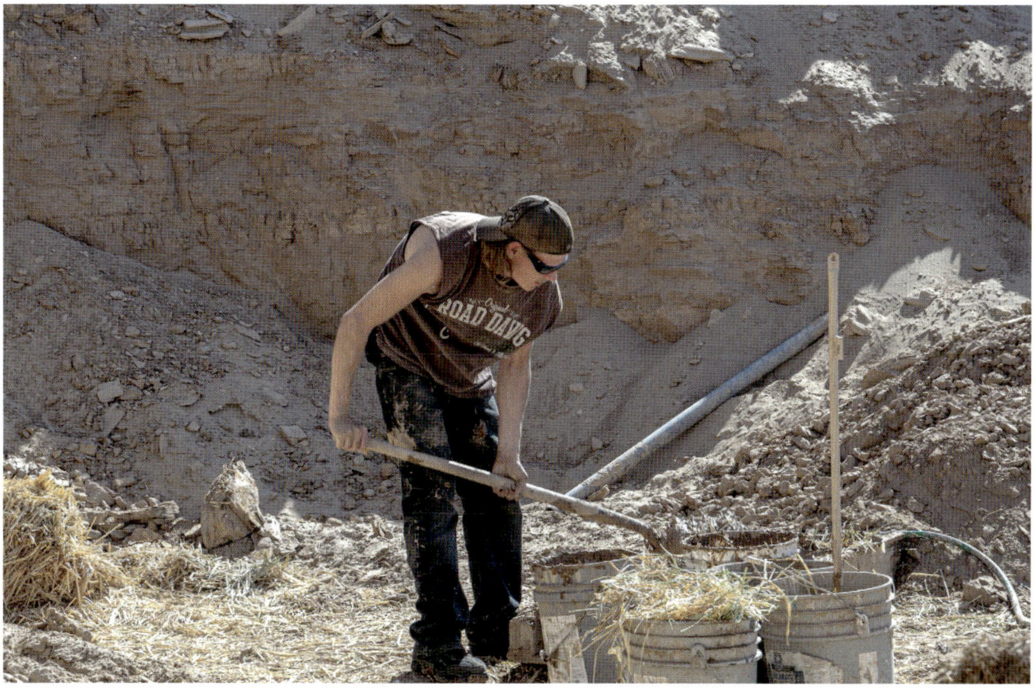

VOLUNTEER: Volunteers assist with the expansion of the mountain's footprint and its maintenance, including repairs and applications of donated paint.

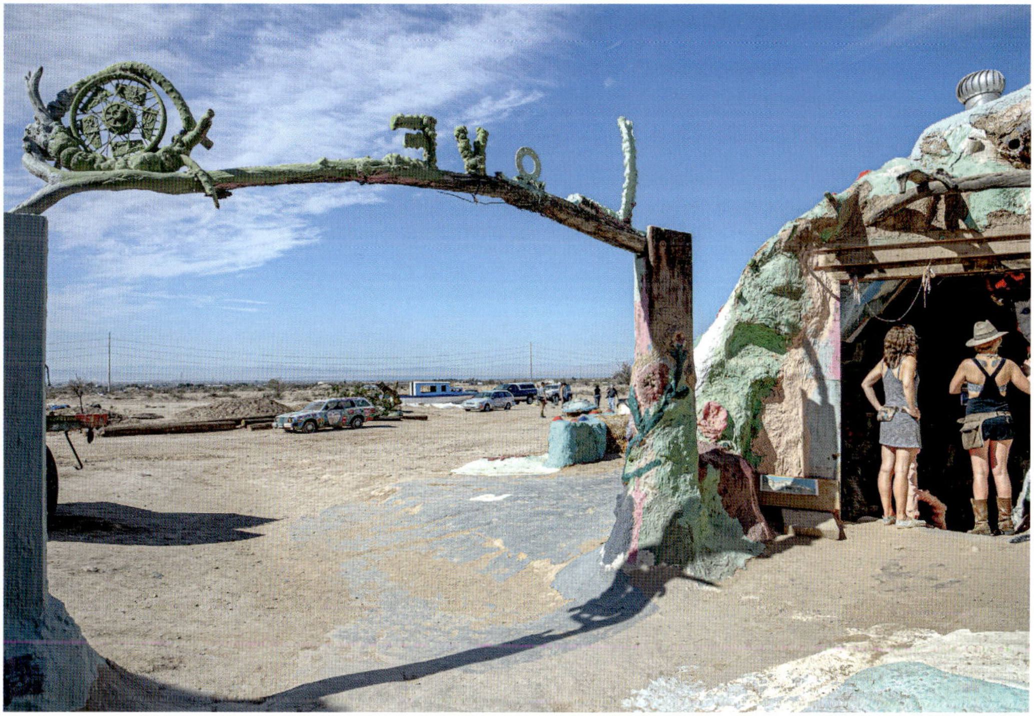

ENTRANCE TO MOUNTAIN INTERIOR AND SHRINE ON RIGHT: In 1998, Knight built a Hogan—a dome-shaped structure that resembled Navajo architecture. The Hogan is attached to the mountain.

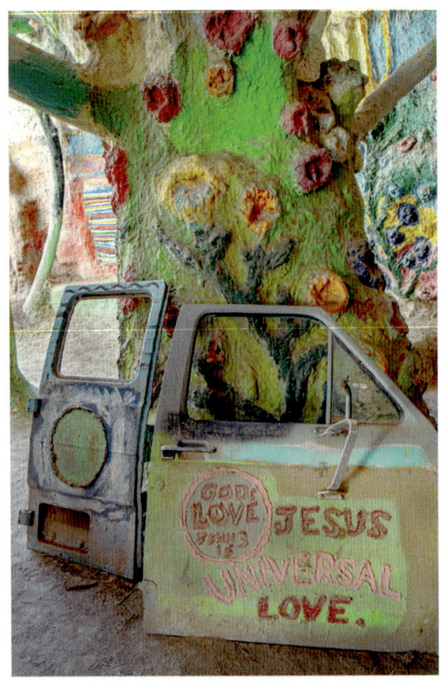

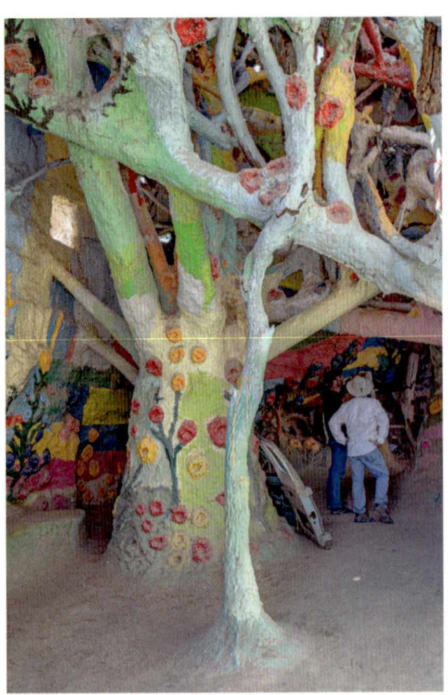

◀ **INTERIOR OF MUSEUM:** The museum is supported by paint-coated trees and tires.

▶ **MUSEUM PASSAGEWAY:** Knight's message is Christian, but it is a non-denominational and straightforward message: God is love.

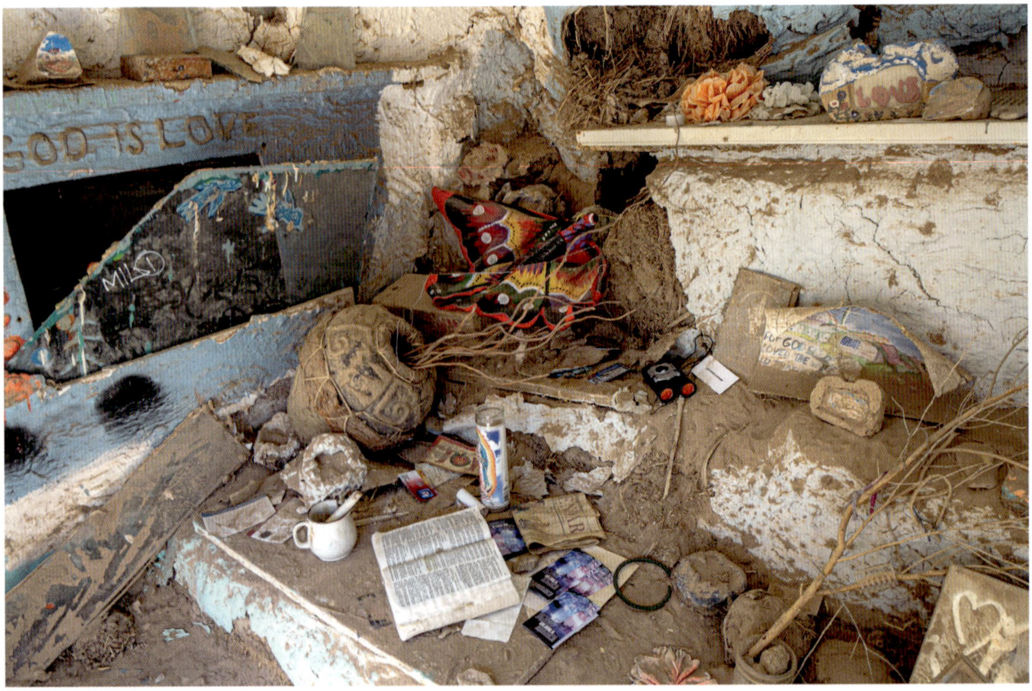

SHRINE: Many make pilgrimages to Salvation Mountain and leave trinkets and notes at the small mountain shrine.

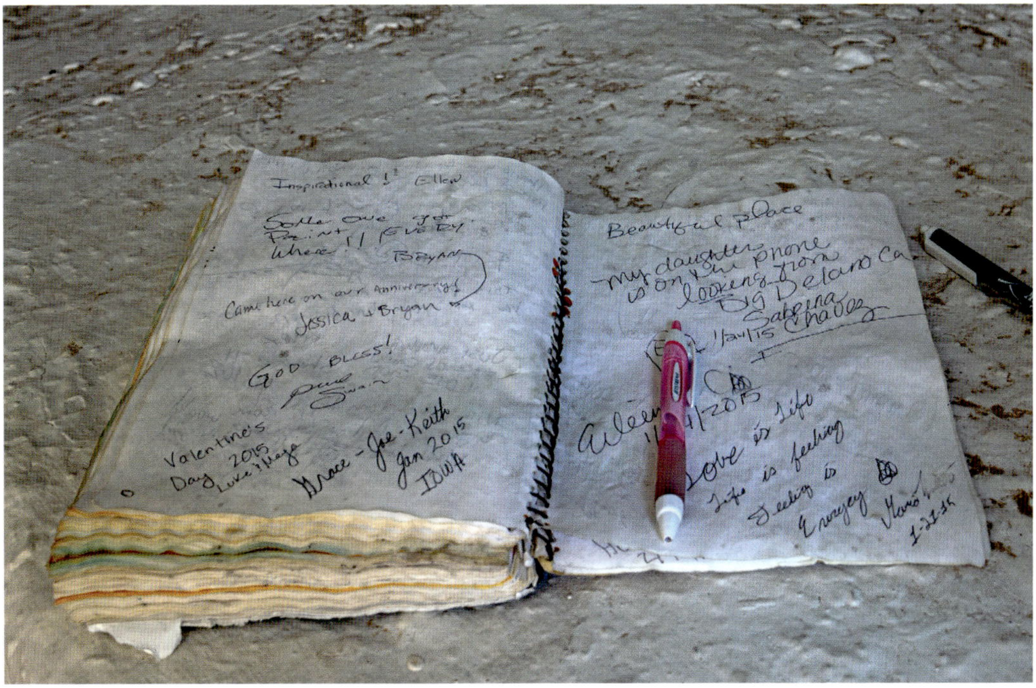

GUEST BOOK: A guest book rests within the mountain shrine room and allows visitors to register comments about inspiration and their journeys to the site.

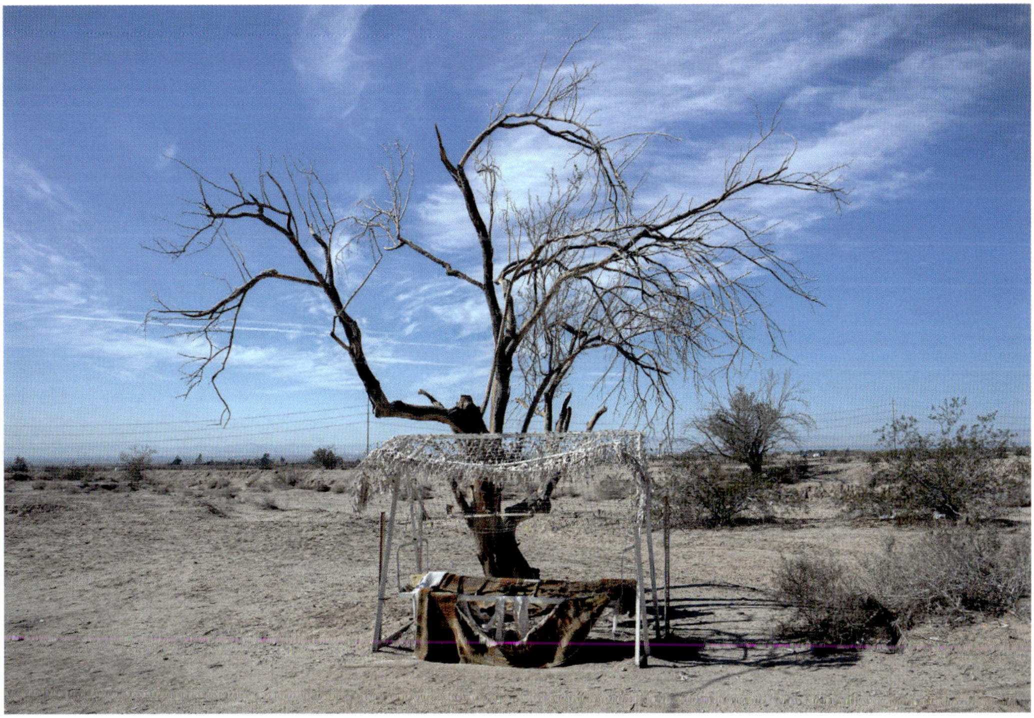

HAVE A SEAT: A hammock is situated under a dead tree at the bottom of Salvation Mountain and behind Knight's van/home.

4

THE ATTRACTION OF NOWHERE:
ABANDONED CONFORMITY, PART I

From my perch on the Salvation Mountaintop, my first view of Slab City looked like a Mad Max wasteland movieset with its haphazardly positioned vehicles, scattered debris, and swarms of dust kicking up when a vehicle took motion. Slab City is a free domain—a haven for those wanting to live off the grid. One would think such a community would be lawless, Mad Max-esque style, but Slab turf rules prevail, and there are consequences for those that break them. Driving through the Slab neighborhood is eye-opening with its unique societal structure. I think the people living here are ready for the apocalypse and have a survival edge on all of us if that doomed time ever greets our world.

Slab City is odd and simultaneously enthralling. Before I visited the Slab, I remembered a few telling me to avoid it because it is dangerous and anarchic. Believe me, as an urban explorer, I dropped into far more perilous places than the Slab. This scrubby desert patch of free spirits, rebels, rule-abhorrent nonconformists, and most likely several societal misfits seem quite content with their order—or lack of order. Observing the Slab territory flooded my mind with 1960s hippie-era nostalgia. Slab City is such a unique environment that many identify as home. Thousands of snowbirds migrate to the Slab during the winter, and a few hard-core Slabbers remain full-time residents.

The California desert's Slab City, built on the footprint of the abandoned World War II Marine military base, Camp Dunlap, plucks its name from the old concrete foundations remaining after the base closed and deconstructed the military structures. Slab City does not have modern conveniences—no power lines, no irrigation, and obviously, no trash pickup service. I saw several generators and solar panel set-ups to compensate for the lack of modern utilities. I also saw many intermediate caged bulk containers for water collection. Initially, my focus was locked on the Slab's significant quantities of refuse, some precariously built huts, and so many vehicles on cement blocks or simply those without tires and slumped into the ground. Many Slabbers marked their living boundaries with empty beer bottles or pieces of glass by pushing them into the earth for make-shift fencing. While the Slab is lawless in a governmental rule-sense, commonality policies prevail. The Slab holds its own rules and selects a leader from the core community of long-term Slabbers to oversee the Slab order. If one does not follow the Slab rules, one is banished from the district. Several sub-communities appear within or adjacent to the Slab City footprint—some cater to religious orientations, and others are pockets for creatives, like East Jesus, while another is the introverted West Satan enclave displaying bold warning signs to visitors not to enter their space—or else.

Money does not seem to hold great importance within the Slab, and unfortunately, many Slabbers live in poverty, but some residents, nevertheless, possess affluent means. Yes, a few physicians, lawyers, veterinarians, corporate executives, and bankers live in the Slab. Swapping and bartering are standard practices for those holding wealth or not. The Slab even has its pirate radio station. The Slab also has a river shower basin for bathing, a few food services, a library, an internet-equipped hostel, and a few places that partake in Airbnb services. I read that Amazon even delivers to the Slab even though the area does not have a registered address.

I was captivated by this lifestyle. To be free and fanciful and to establish a house without restraint is quite an attractive option—no homeowners association restrictions, no property taxes, no camping fees, and definitely no "keeping up with the Joneses." Living within a society that has your back is a big bonus too. I am not sure I could tolerate the summer heat, though, when temperatures rise to 120 degrees and greater, and I doubt even more if I could live a comfortable life without electricity or a genuine working shower. How would I computer-edit my photographs that demand endless hours of focused concentration? Like the mirages of nature's glory on some Salton Sea beaches, Slab City might be a mirage for easy constraint-free living.

Sadly, California is on a path to sell Slab City property—perhaps a sale to energy companies that can exploit the dry land's minerals. The residents of Slab City are attempting to purchase the Slab land to keep their squatting status whole. Of course, a Slab acquisition of property will thrust the community into a landlord-tenant class, and does not this run contrary to the culture of Slab living? Still, only Slab baby steps are required now—secure the land with a purchase from donations and worry about the ownership status and rules after the fact. Seeing how resourceful and resilient the Slabbers are, I am sure they will generate a solution to their dilemma and avoid a property seizure from the California government, yet somehow maintain their beloved abandonment of conformity. After all, if any group is apocalypse-ready, the Slabbers hold this crown and certainly will overcome more silly rules about real estate standing.

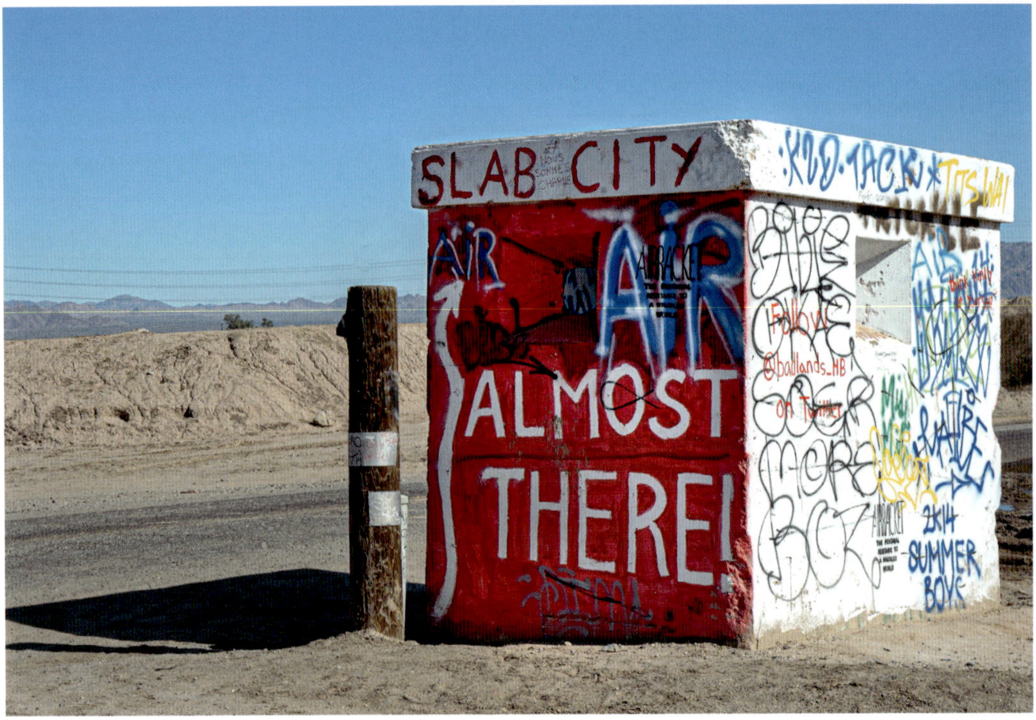

SLAB CITY ENTRANCE: In the middle of the California desert is Slab City—a community where all can live off-the-grid.

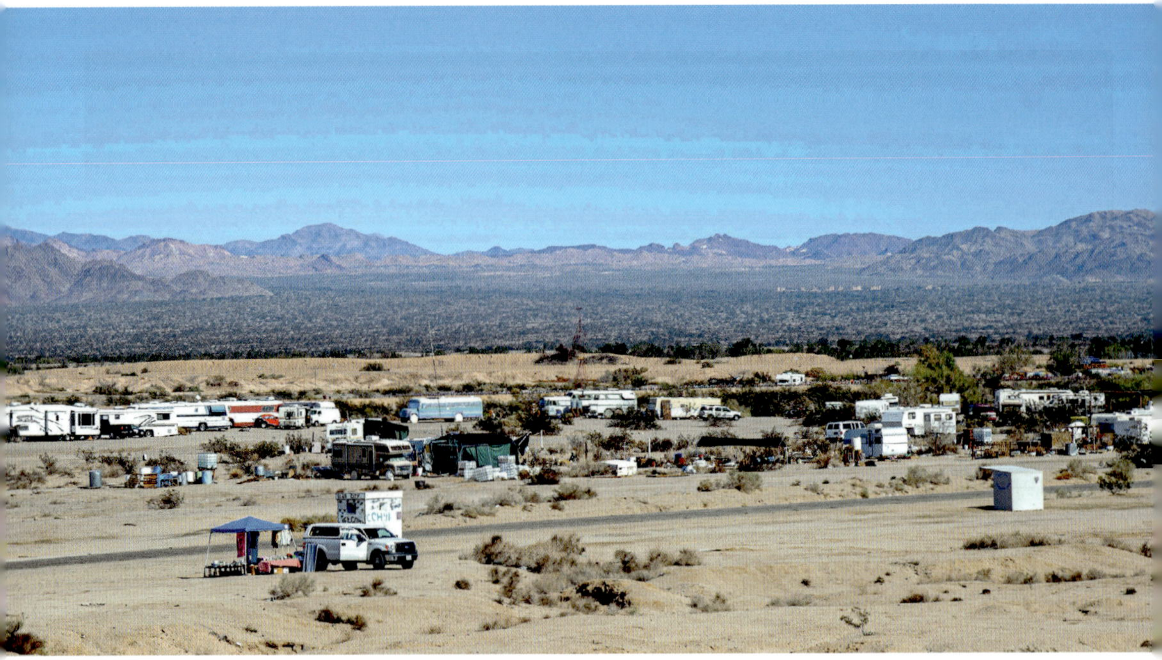

VIEW OF SLAB CITY FROM TOP OF SALVATION MOUNTAIN: Slab City is not only composed of professionals such as doctors, veterinarians, and lawyers, but also mavericks, rogues, free spirits, anarchists, and strong individualists.

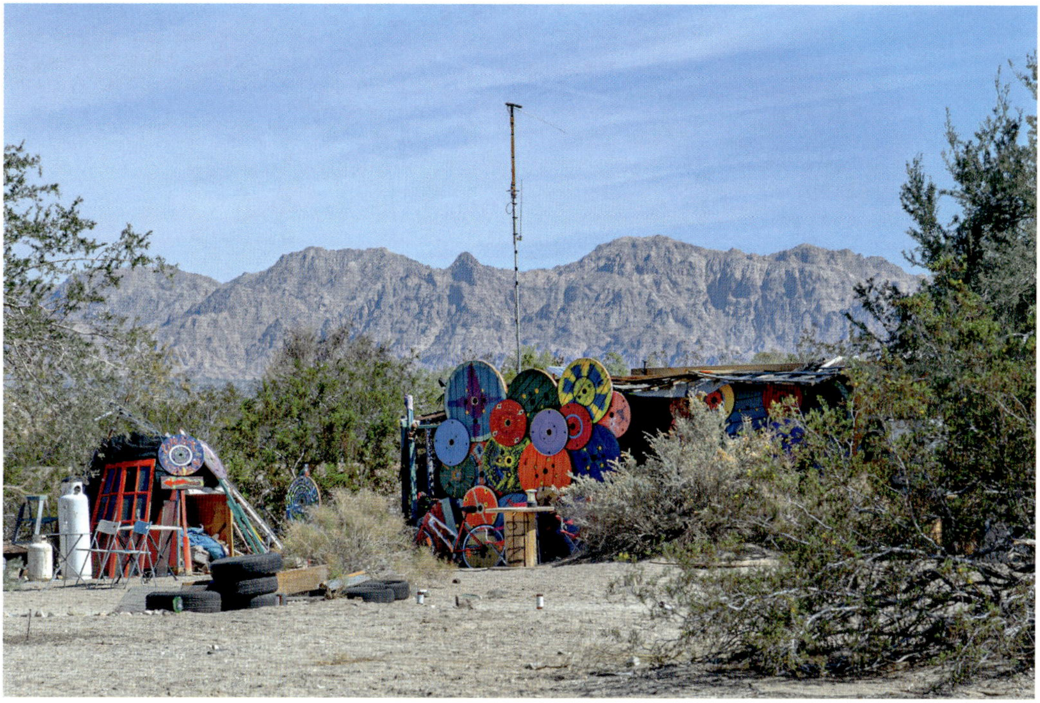

DWELLING: Slab City derived its name from the military base Camp Dunlop foundations that remained post-demolition.

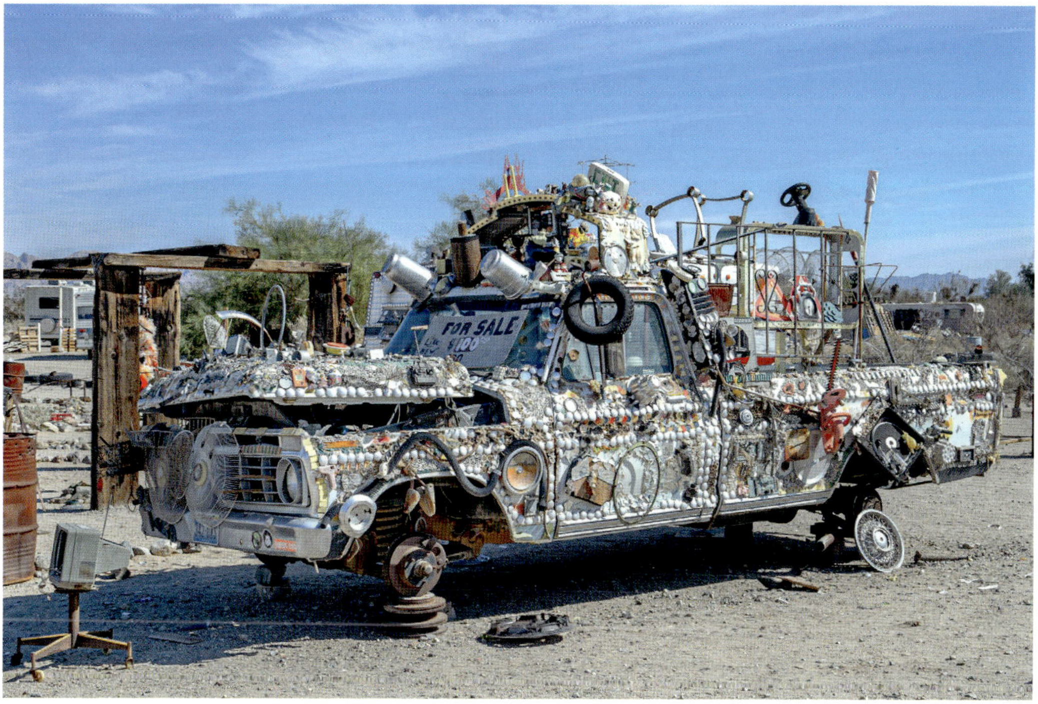

ARTISTIC CREATION: A Slab resident presents artistic expression to a truck and has a $100 OBO sale sign affixed to the windshield.

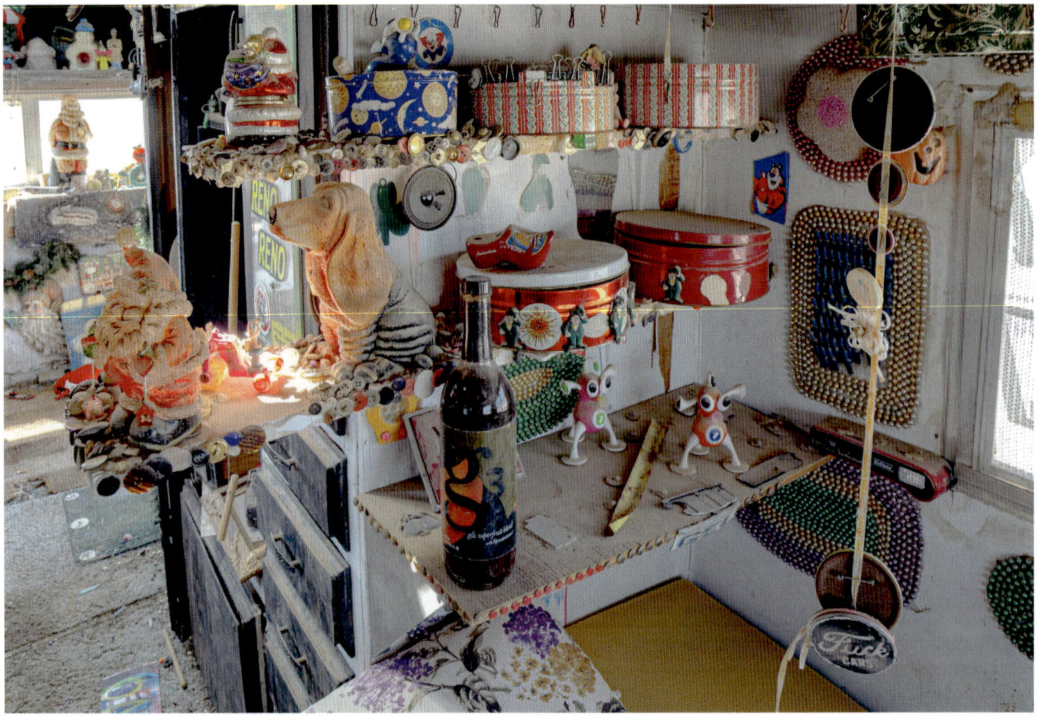

CAMPER INTERIOR: Slab City is primarily a winter destination for snowbirds, but several remain as permanent residents. Summer temperatures can exceed 120 degrees.

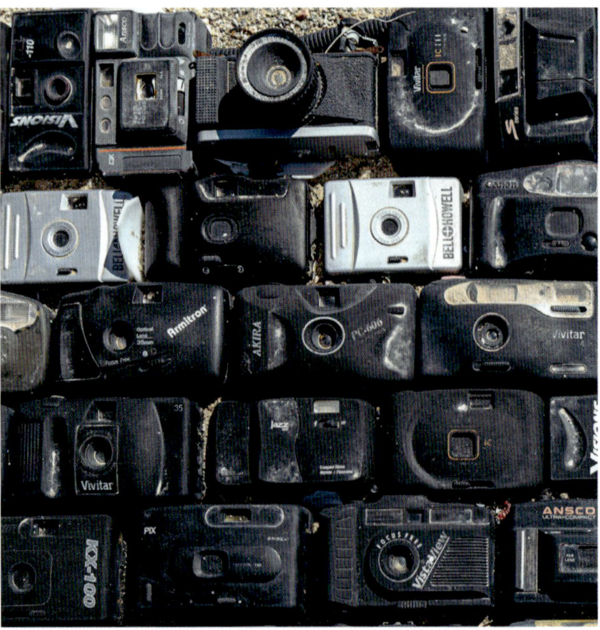

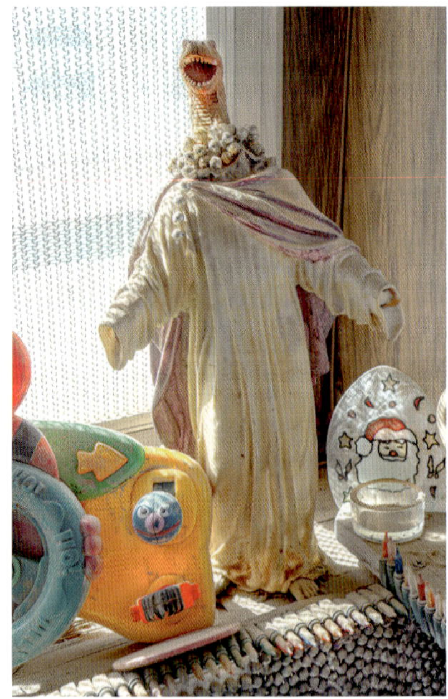

◀ **SLAB ART:** Slab City holds does not possess any utilities, including water and electrical services.

▶ **CAMPER INTERIOR:** Shortly after Camp Dunlop was conveyed to the state of California, squatters assembled at the site and called it home.

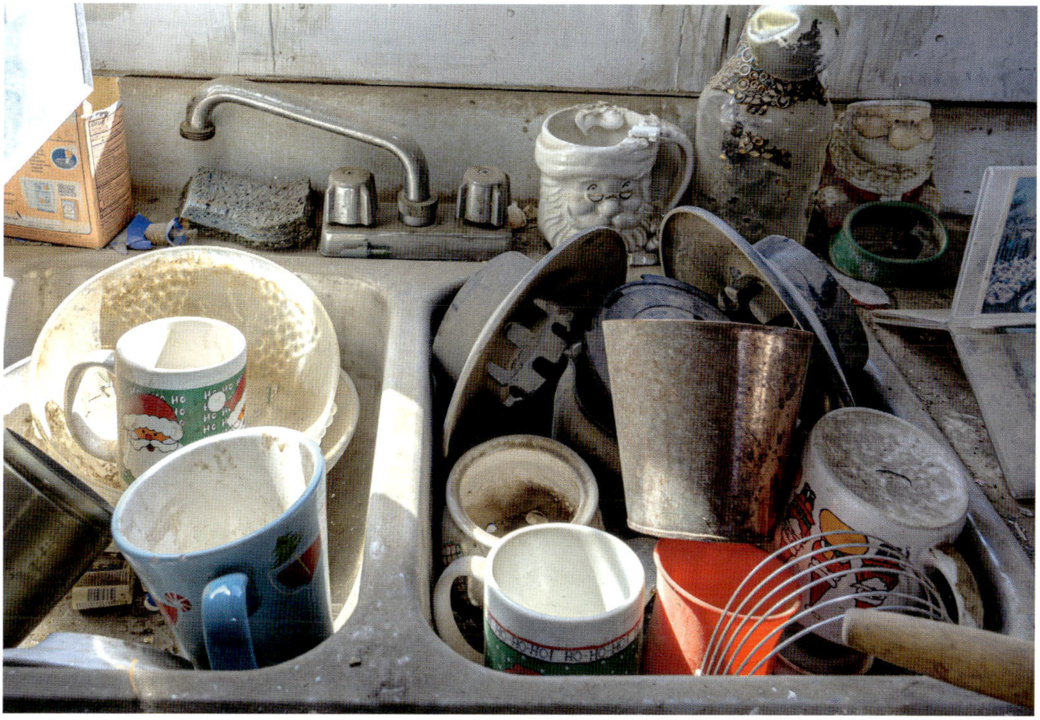

CAMPER INTERIOR: There are many sub-communities within the Slab, and the groups appeal to diverse interests.

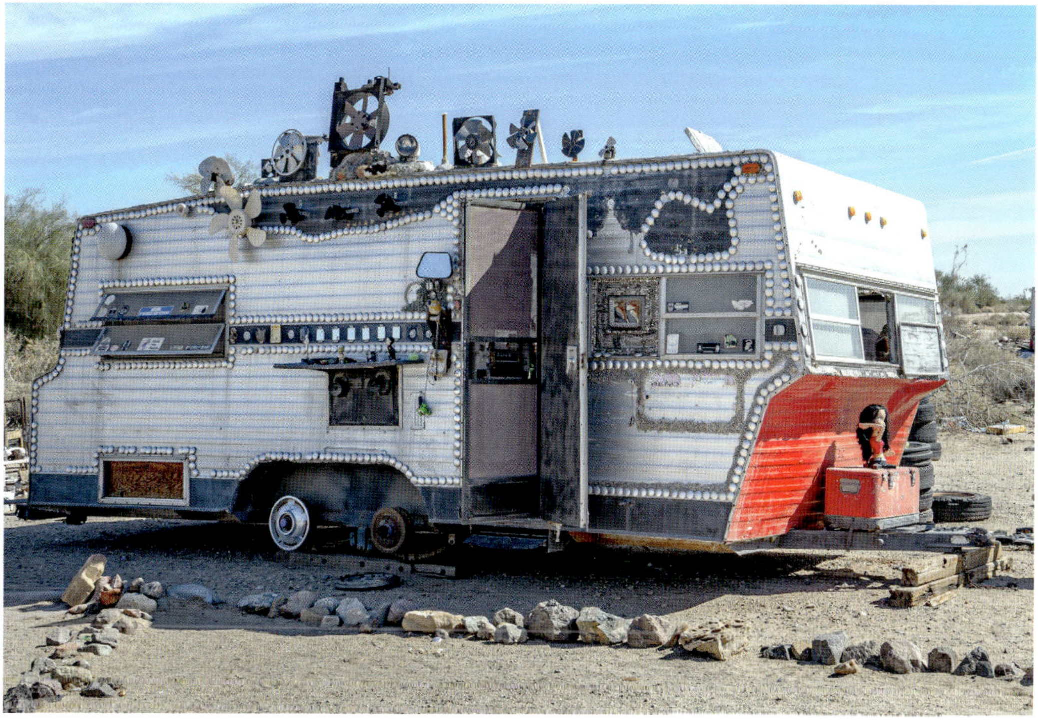

A SLAB DWELLING: The long-term Slabbers dictate the community's rules, and violations of the rules can result in banishment from the Slab.

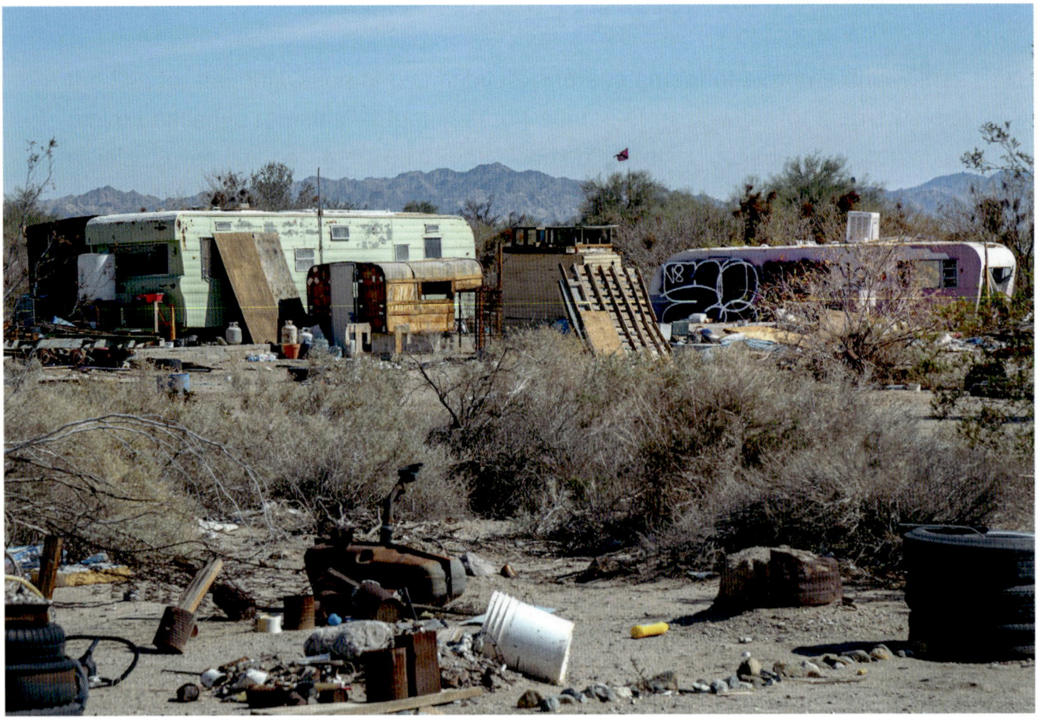

SLAB NEIGHBORS: Bartering for services and goods is common in the Slab.

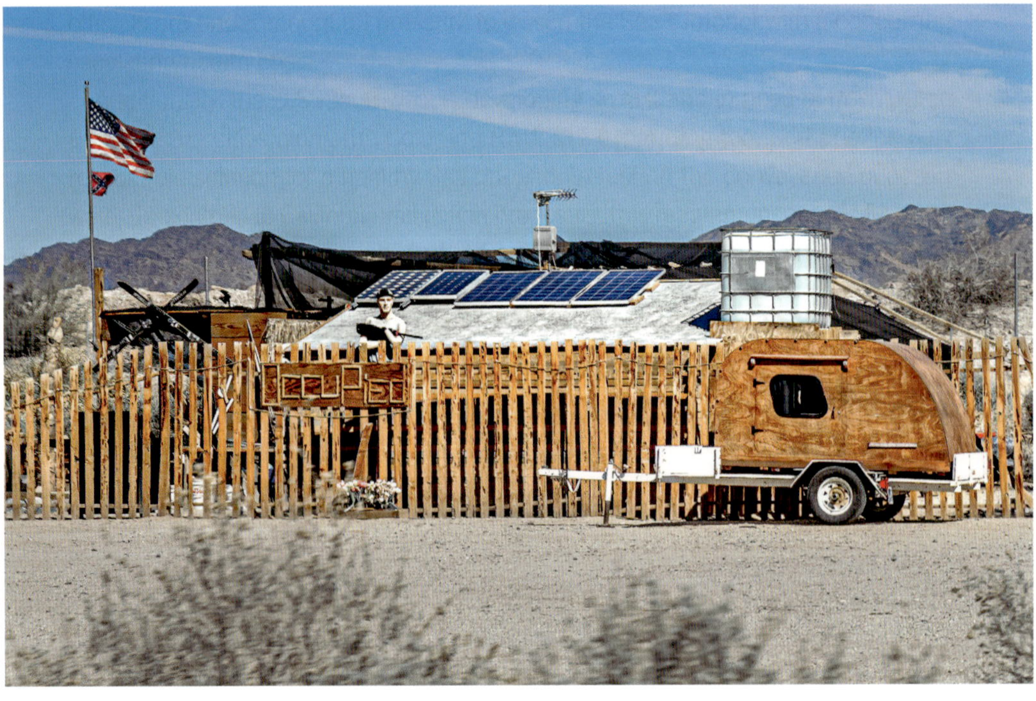

OCCUPIED: An elaborate solar and antenna array is featured on this Slab dwelling. The mannequin holding the assault rifle and the "Occupied" sign does not present an inviting appearance.

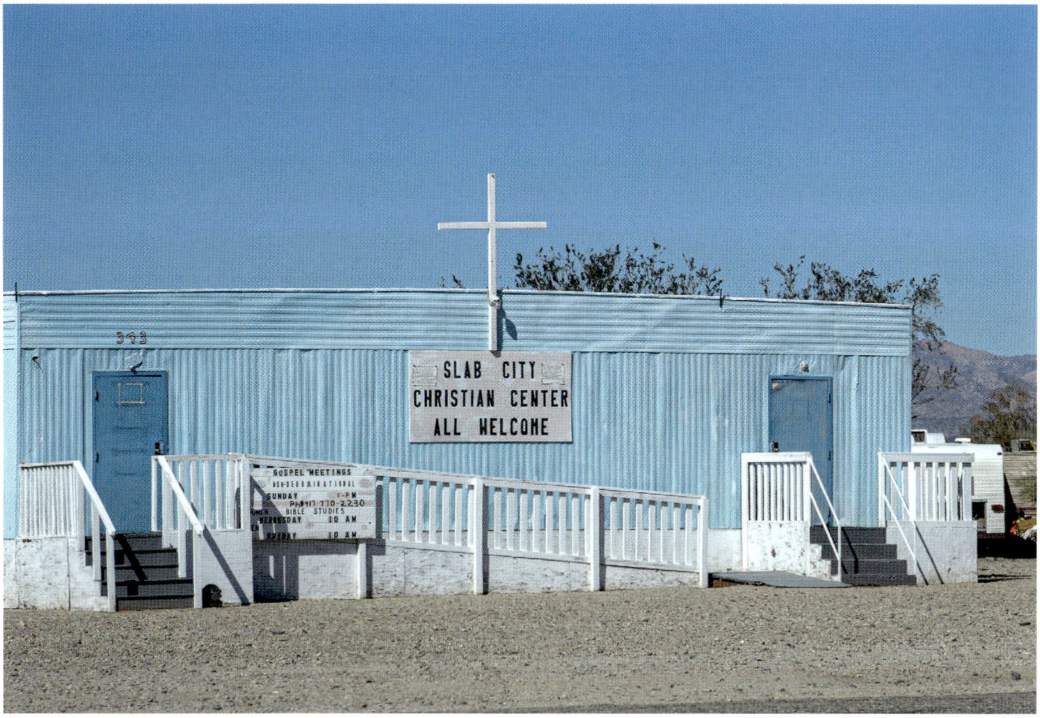

CHRISTIAN CENTER: Amazon makes deliveries to Slab City even though Slab residents do not have official addresses.

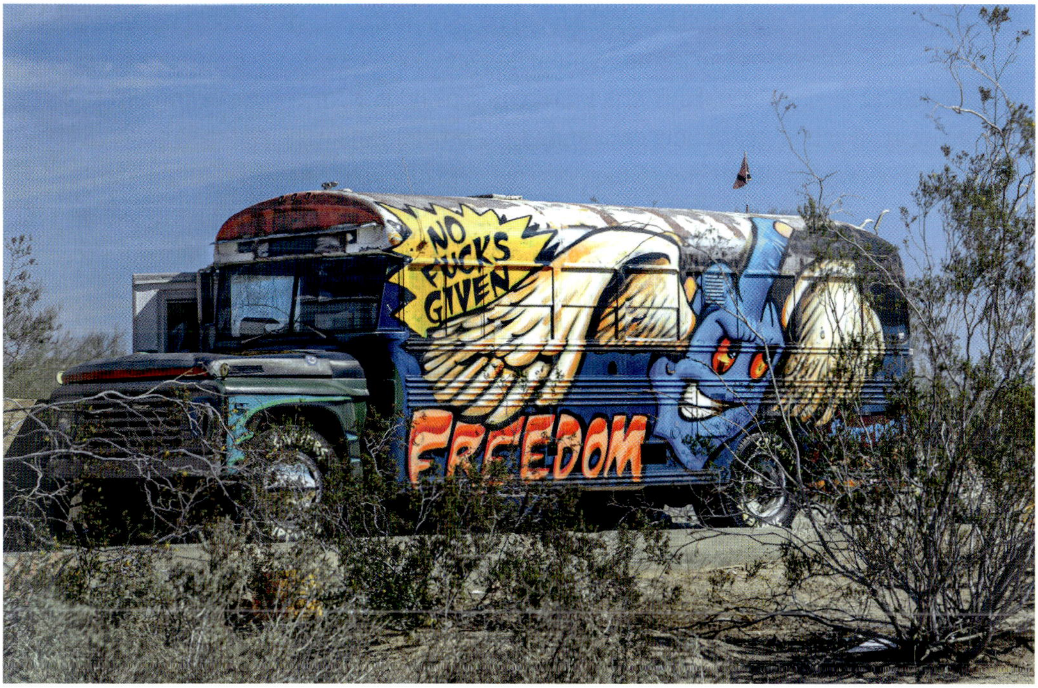

DWELLING: A river shower is available for bathing, and the Slab offers other services such as internet in a hostel.

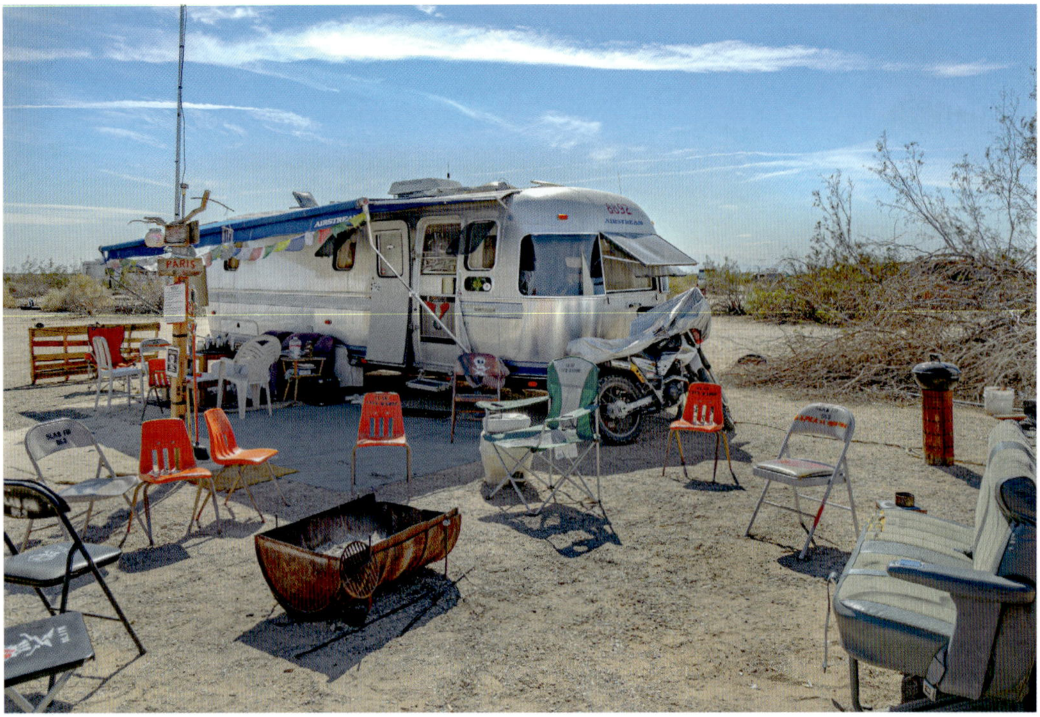

RADIO STATION: A New York artist operates a Slab pirate radio station from a fully-equipped, solar-powered 1995 Airstream. An open-air tiki bar next to the Airstream is a bonus.

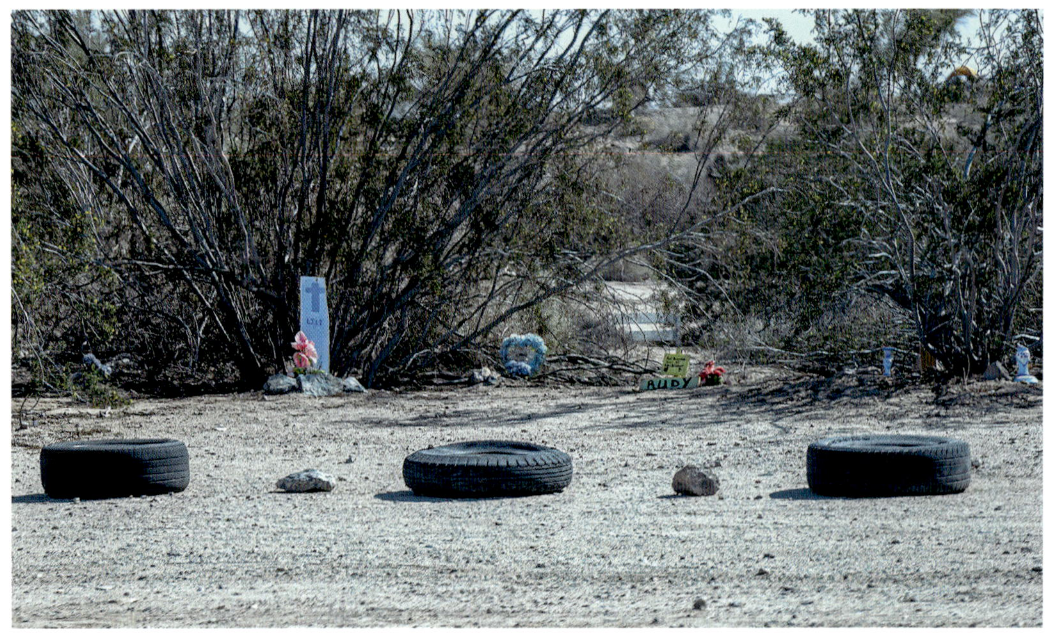

PET CEMETERY: Small memorials designate the burial spots for some beloved Slab pets.

5

A PLACE IN THE MIDDLE OF NOWHERE: ABANDONED CONFORMITY, PART II

Like Walter Knight, another visionary, Charles Russell (1965-2011), cooked the creative juices to establish the artists' enclave, East Jesus. East Jesus is stationed within the greater Slab City footprint. At first blush, with Salvation Mountain as a neighbor, the East Jesus moniker implies a religious slant for this collective. Nonetheless, as an East Jesus representative told me, the name means a place in the middle of nowhere—indeed, it is. This eclectic site is filled with distinctive and eccentric art installations created entirely from trash and recycled materials—nothing is discarded, and all refuse is repurposed.

In 2007, Russell, an engineer, abandoned his technology job and headed to Slab City. Russell intended to serve as a Salvation Mountain volunteer but refocused his attention on artistic endeavors and inaugurated the first steps toward the creation of the prolific East Jesus community. In short order, an array of structures for "living" appeared, courtesy of Russell's engineering expertise and handicraft. Soon, several art pilgrims established their nonconformist roots at this homesite.

Upon passing through the East Jesus entrance art arch, one observes exceptional community order, and unlike Slab City, this fascinating sector holds a private property status. The non-profit Chasterus Foundation, a tag honoring Russell, purchased the 30-acre East Jesus plot in 2016. Just as someone would assume from a place called East Jesus, warmth and congeniality abound. All are welcome, and a community representative was proud to show off the hamlet's outdoor art museum and lifestyle. The colorful art entryway dazzles with a profusion of artistry, including a massive alligator formed with thousands of white plastic retail bags, a curvy high wall made of concrete and bottles, and other creations prompting profound contemplation.

One of my favorite art installations is a stacked bank of televisions graffitied with introspective statements about media's effect on our society. The amusing art cars of the late Mr. Russell still hold court in the museum's garden of delights. Behind East Jesus's open-air gallery is the residence area where a maze of trailers, vans, and buses surround the common living areas. Shared features include a geodesic dome for growing plants and vegetables, a library, a space for music jams, an internet access portal, a pantry, a recycling area, a kitchen, and a patio where many residents and pets mingled on upholstered couches. Gender specified lavatories feature a shovel and bucket of manure for the earth toilets' final step after one finishes their "business." East Jesus hums well on solar power. East Jesus also has its very own town planner—a caretaker for the collective. This off-the-grid micro village hopes to expand some of its community practices to benefit the Slab as a whole. For example, East Jesus is active in enlisting county and state grants for the acquisition of Slab dumpsters to alleviate the Slab's compounding litter problem.

I thoroughly enjoyed my tour of East Jesus and the attractiveness of a simple pretentious-free life. The cooperative was orderly and offered many services—I especially liked the pink hair salon. I can imagine lively music gigs at night and the joyful process of crafting art masterpieces from broken appliances, tin cans, and assorted junk. It must be nice that this little section of inventive paradise is free from land seizure too, but I wonder how the collective residents feel about taxes—someone has to pay them now, yes? The collective has a small retail section, too, and offers fan merch. I purchased an East Jesus t-shirt, so perhaps these sales assist with their property tax payments. The East Jesusites better not get too comfortable with structure, though, because rules and rigidity might weaken the survival skill set. However, I doubt that survival skills will ever be problematic for East Jesus residents given the remarkable ingenuity of this community. Oh yeah, one last thing: the East Jesus representative warned us to stay away from their adjacent neighbor and another sub-Slab community, West Satan, as they do not welcome visitors—such is the yin and yang of communal living.

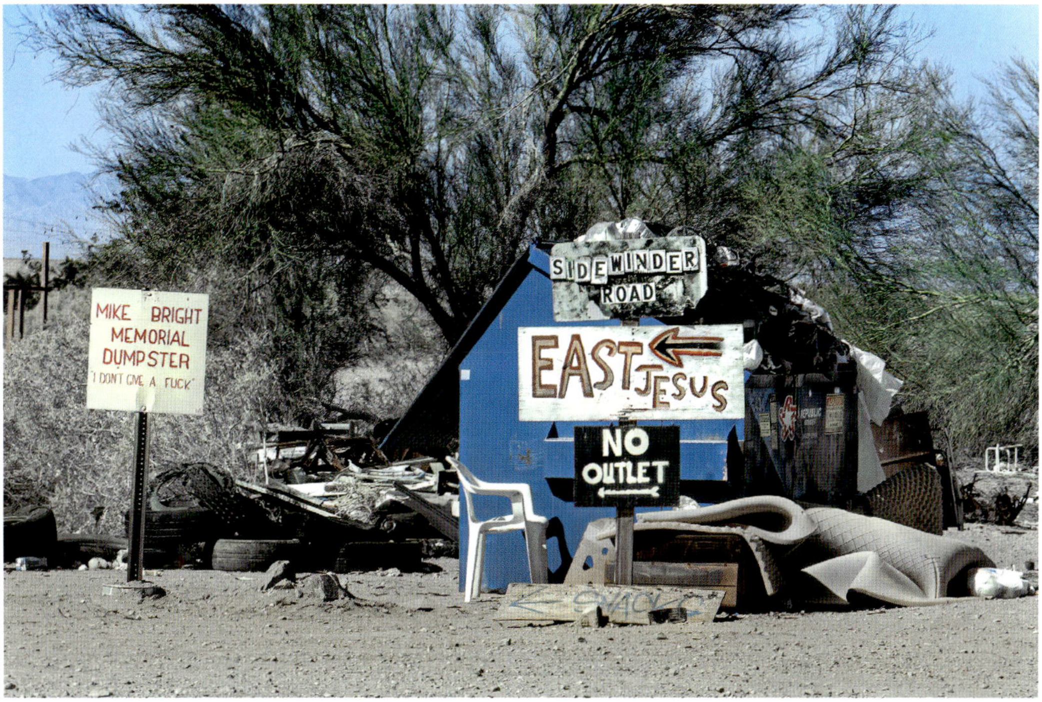

DIRECTIONAL SIGN FOR EAST JESUS: East Jesus is an artist community, and is seated at the end of a road within Slab City.

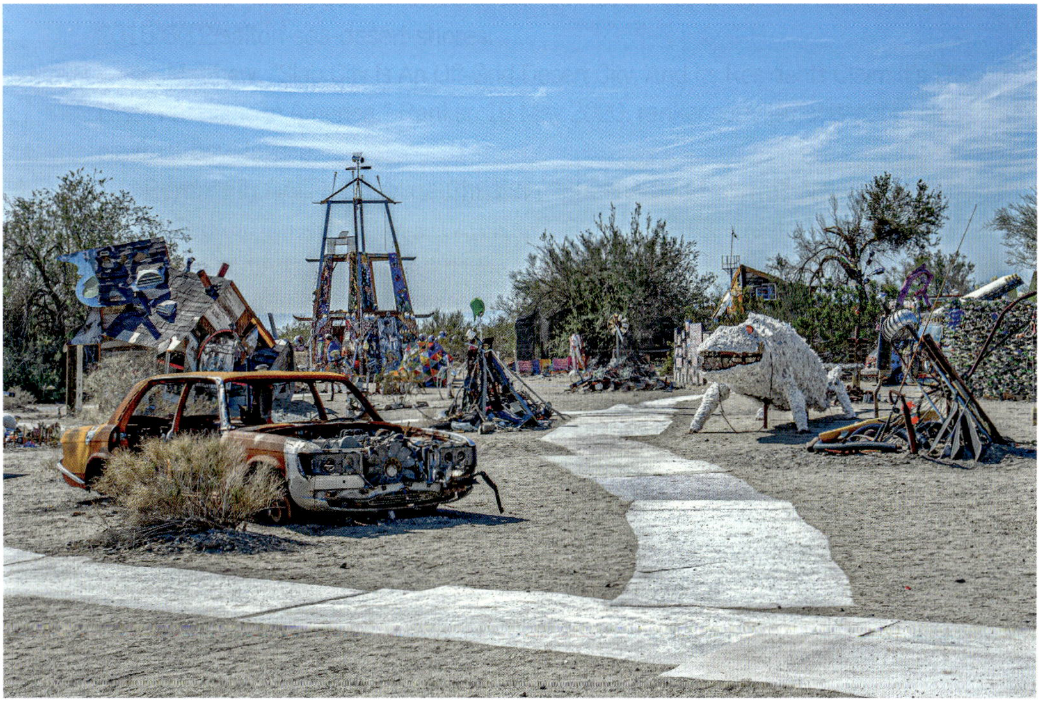

EAST JESUS ENTRANCE AND MUSEUM: East Jesus, a non-religious term, coins its community name from an old Midwest saying when finding oneself off the beaten path, i.e., at East Jesus.

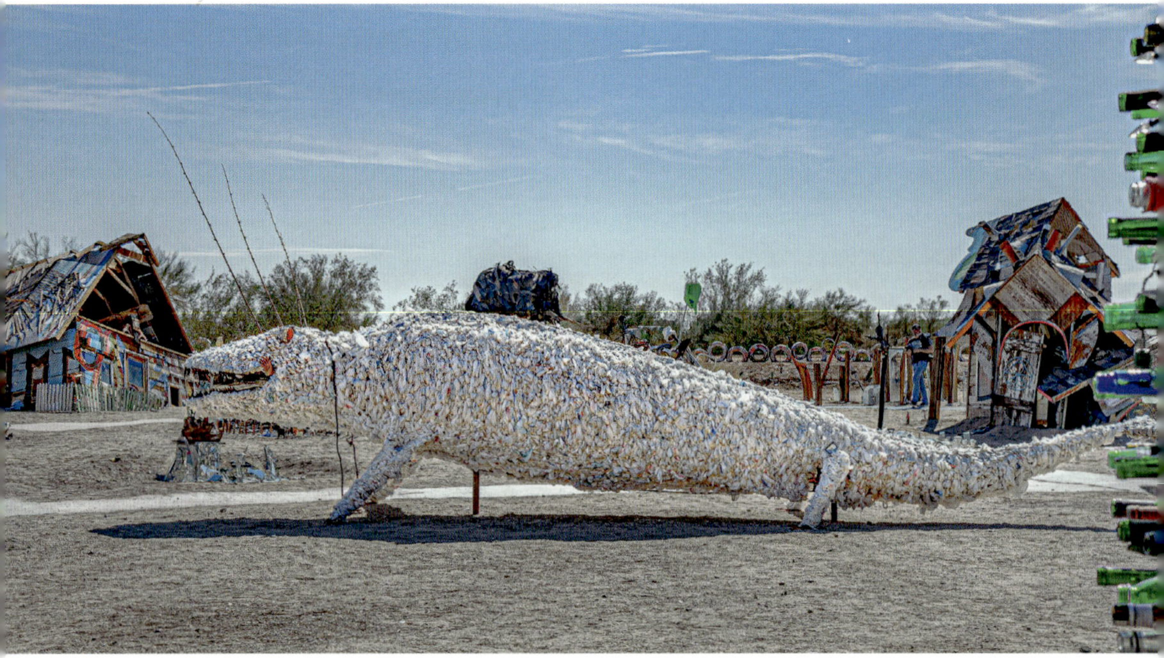

ALBRINO: At the entrance museum is an art installation made from 4,000 plastic bags. "Albrino" was created by resident artist, Royce Carlson.

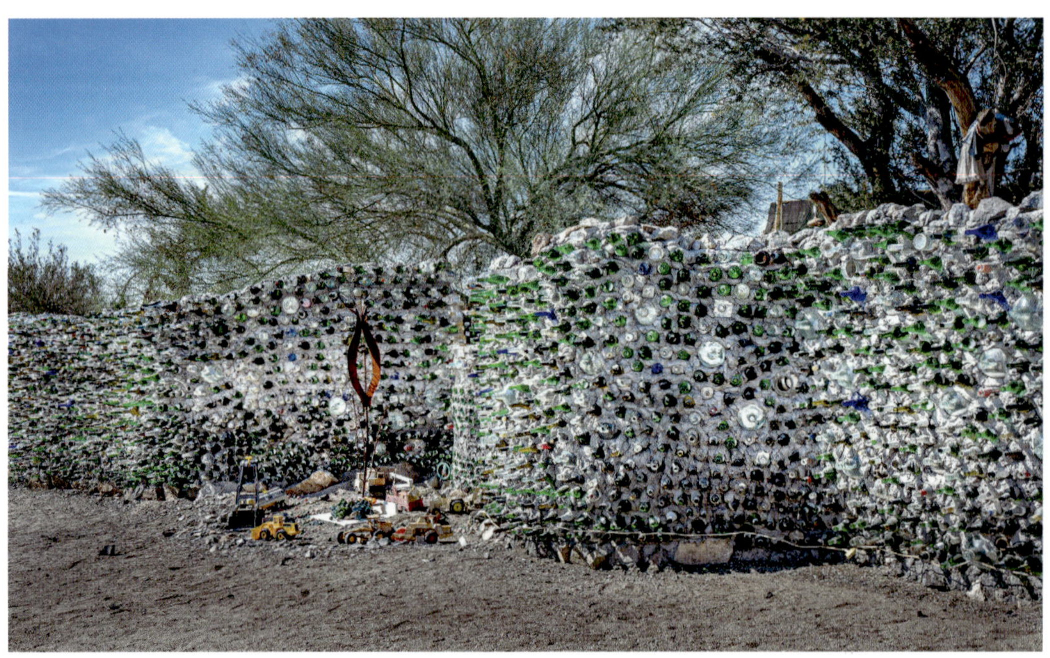

BOTTLE WALL: The heart of the East Jesus community lives behind the curvy wall of bottles. The Bottle Wall is the inspiration of resident artist, Frank Redford.

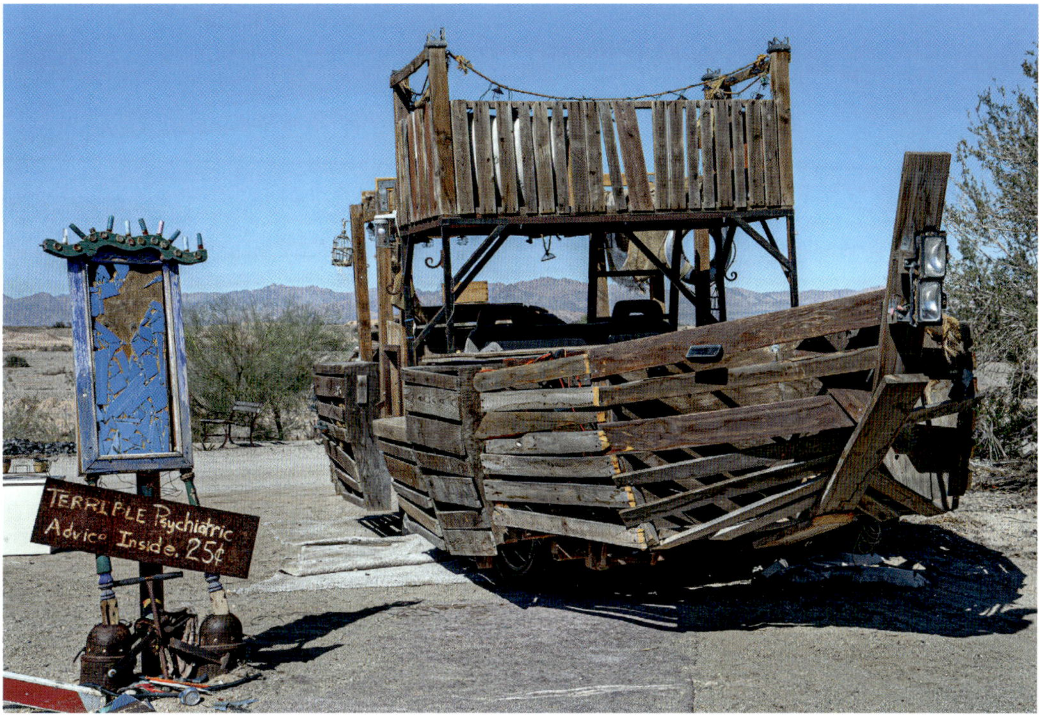

THE DUSTY JUNK: The Dusty Junk, an operational vehicle, is the creation of Shing Yin Khor, Jason Bender, and Scott Keeler. Next to the Junk, a sign advertises terrible psychiatric advice for 25 cents.

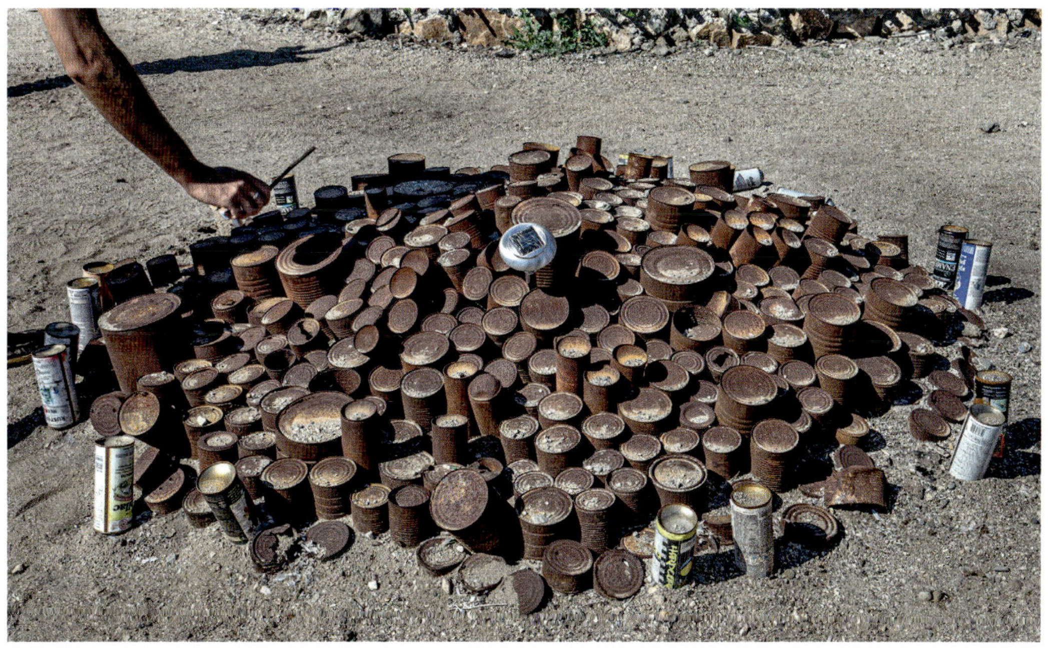

CAN ORGAN: The can organ, constructed by resident artist, Ty Johnson, provides music with stick taps or by dripping water on to the surface.

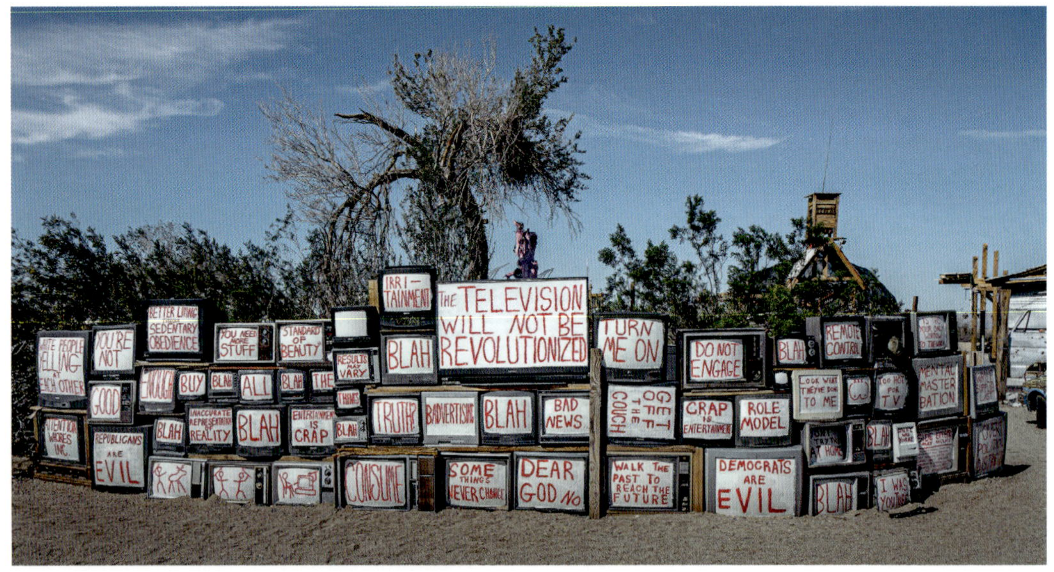

THE TELEVISION WILL NOT BE REVOLUTIONIZED: Resident artist, Flip Cassidy, presents a visual social commentary about media's influence on society.

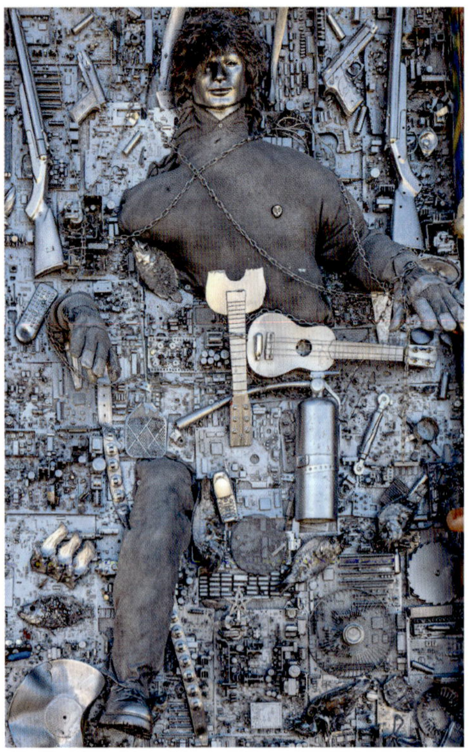

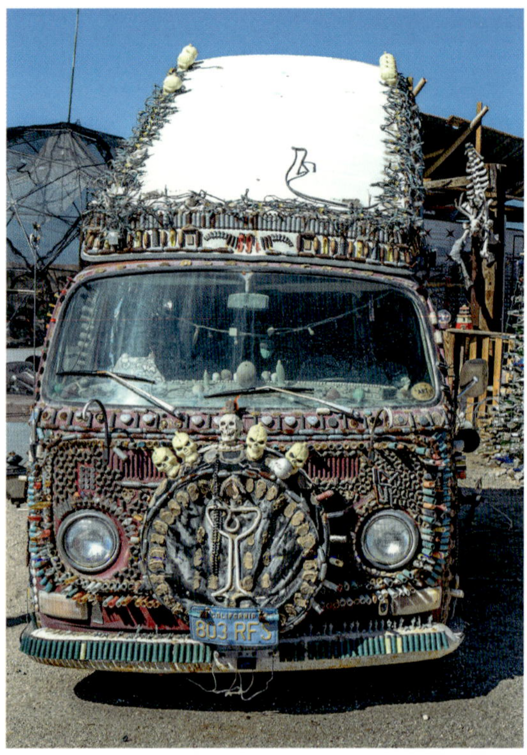

◀ **TOWER OF BARBARELLA:** Resident artist Royce Carlson created the Tower of Barbarella and features several artist contributions, including this "metal" encrusted tower panel.

▶ **CINNABAR CHARM:** The 1971 red Westphalia, Cinnabar Charm, once owned by the late East Jesus founder, Charlie Russell, is a permanent fixture in the outdoor museum.

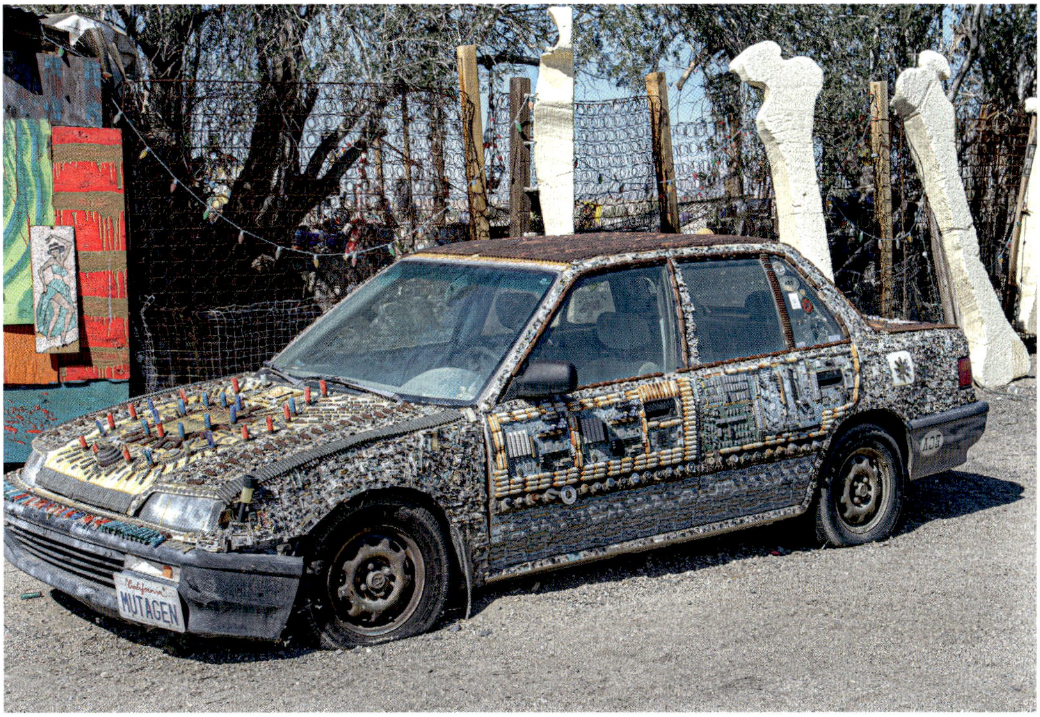

▲ **MUTAGEN:** Russell's other art car, Mutagen, is also an art installation in the East Jesus art garden. The car is adorned with circuit boards, empty nitrous cartridges, bullet shells and other recycled refuse.

▼ **COMMUNITY EARTH TOILET:** East Jesus is unique in that it reuses human manure, "humanure," for fertilizer.

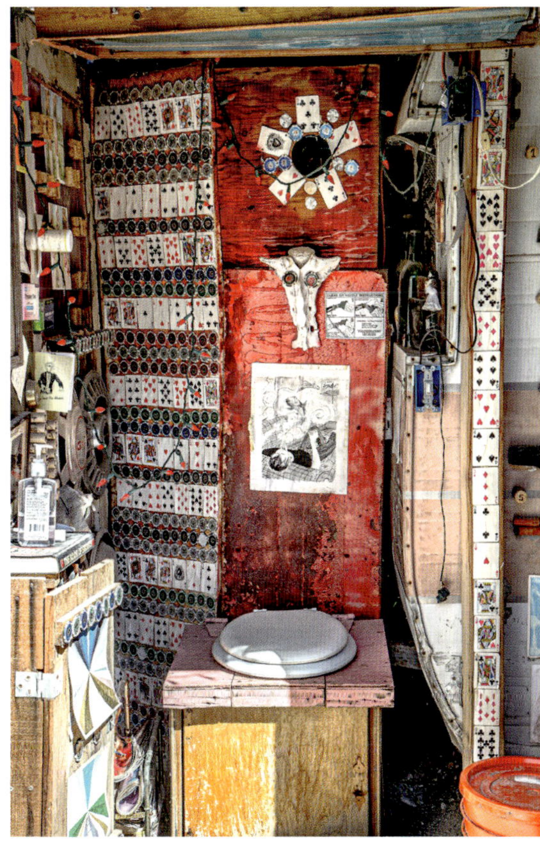

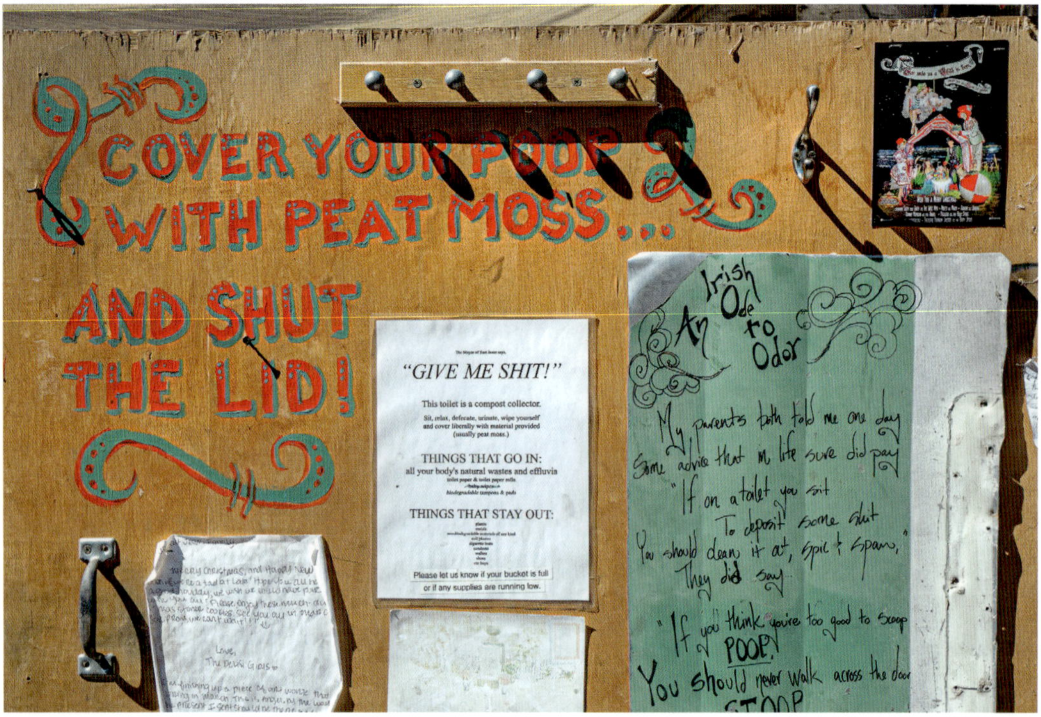

TOILET RULES: "Cover your poop with peat moss and shut the lid."

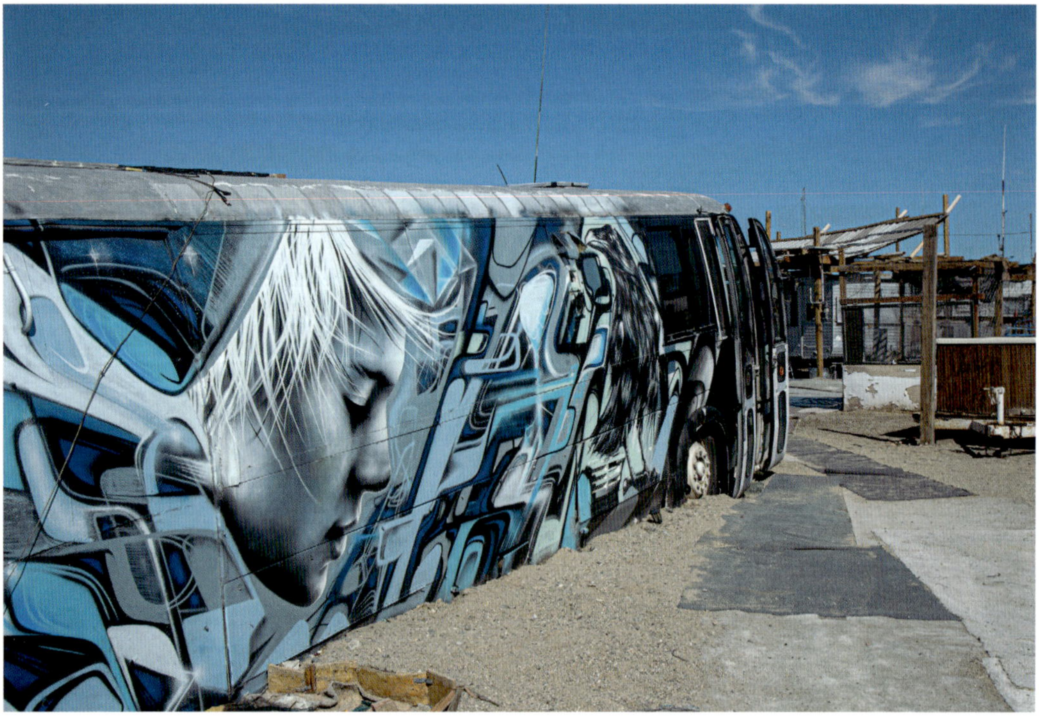

WALTER: This bus wedged in the East Jesus desert sand is named Walter. The mural was created by the artistry of Christina Angelina and Ease One.

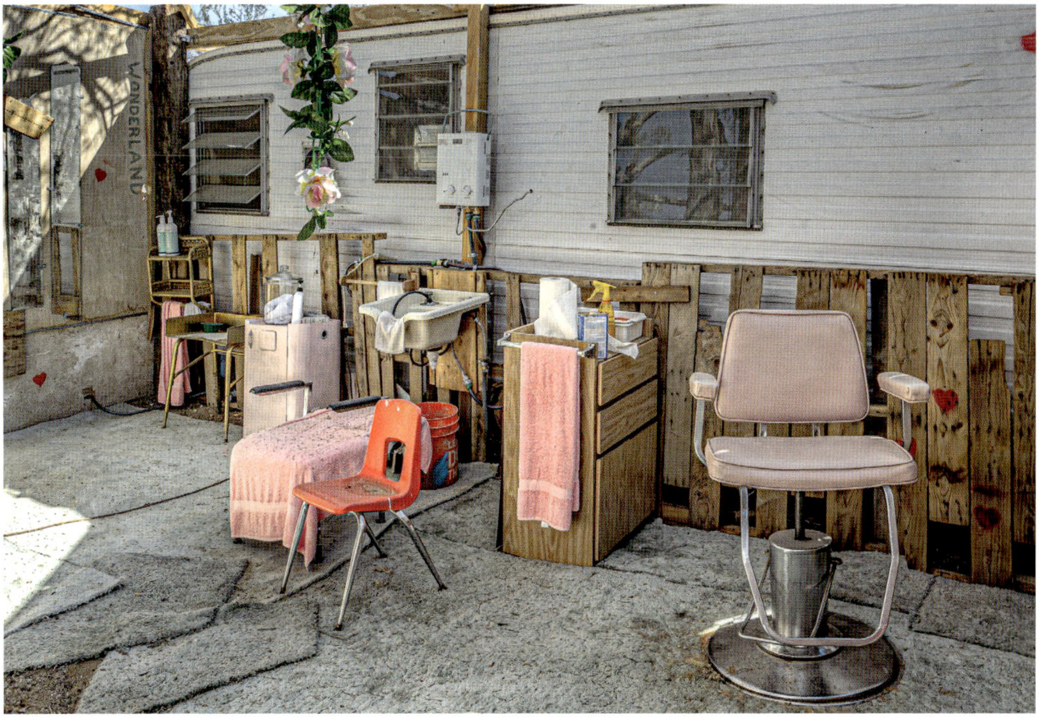

COMMUNITY HAIR SALON: East Jesus has a water distribution system for its residents and common area services.

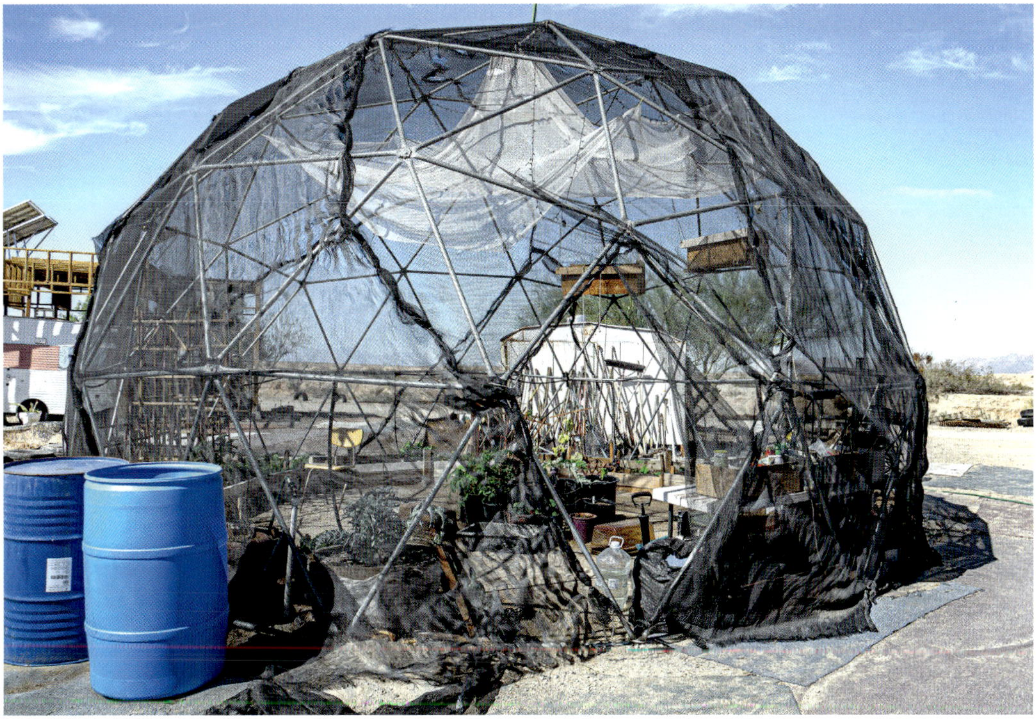

GEODESIC DOME FOR PLANT PROPAGATION: Sustainability projects such as planting crops, fruit trees, composting, and solar array construction are on the East Jesus agenda. East Jesus grows its own food.

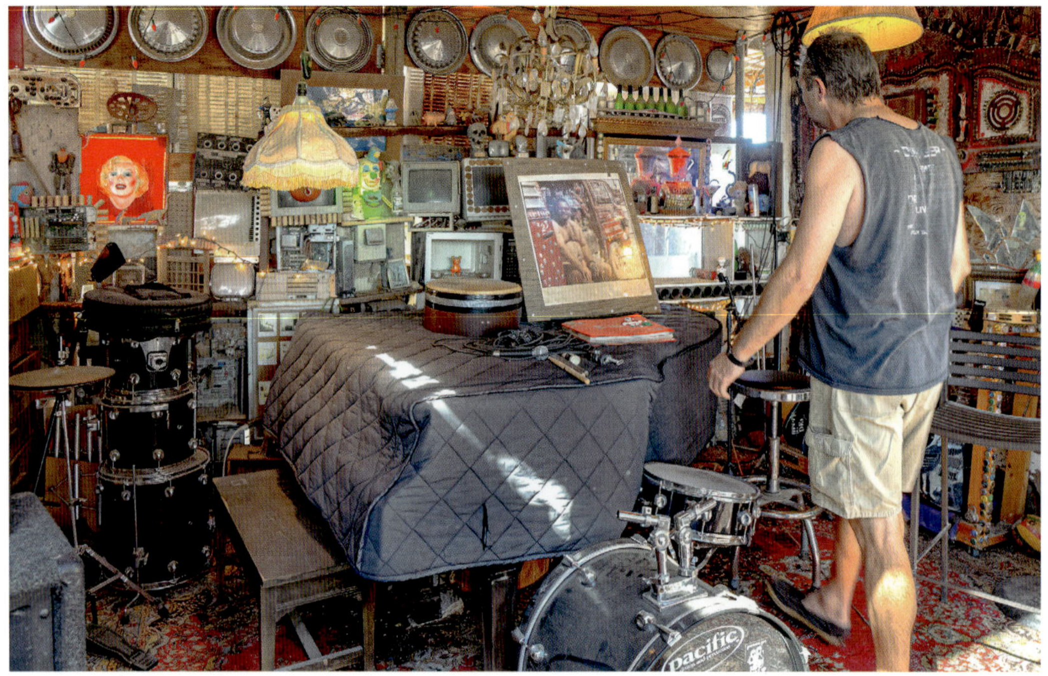

COMMUNITY MUSIC ROOM: A piano, drum set, guitars, and other instruments are available for community jam sessions. The portrait of founder Charles Russell and his cremation ashes hold a place of honor within the music room.

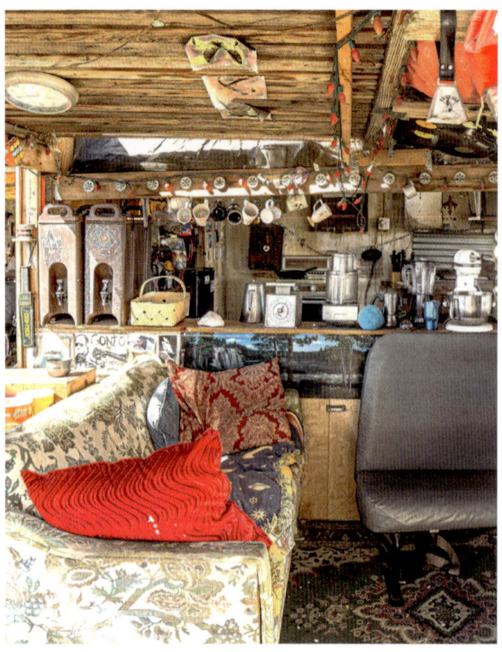

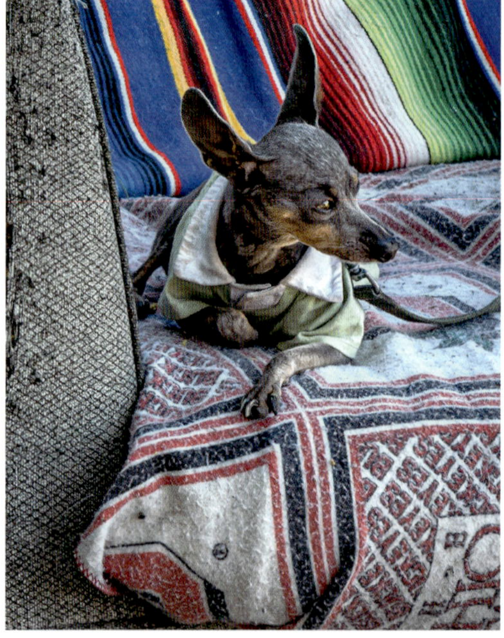

◀ **COMMUNITY KITCHEN:** East Jesus provides a remarkable working model of an improvised community that operates on solar power.

▶ **CHILLIN' IN THE COMMUNITY PATIO:** East Jesus is full of profound, proactive, colorful details, art, residents, and dweller pets.

6

NILE LAND

During America's infancy, many considered themselves residents of the new Athens, or the new Rome—grand spirits for the ages. Thousands of new American towns embraced classical endearments for their novel chapters and in reverential honor toward the great ancient civilizations. In 1914, Niland replaced the sobriquets of Old Beach, Imperial Junction, and Hobgood—handles during Niland's first decade of confusing identity. The crown of Niland was granted by the Imperial Farm Lands Association and based the mark on Africa's Nile lands—also deserts possessing fertile ground. For some time, Niland's crown jewels sparkled with a flourishing agricultural economy and once enjoyed the title of the Tomato Capital of the World. However, like everything in the Salton Sea region, Niland could not escape the ravages of the environmental disaster that hovers over the area like a looming specter. Everywhere one looks, the loss is evident, and Niland is not the exception. Outsourced water gave birth to a new land, but then the water, and then lack of it, brought forth multiple dusty layers of despair—Niland suffers from its Sea cloak.

I always have the same sad feeling whenever I pass through a small town that was once a thriving place, once brimming with life and "busy-ness," but now sits limp, slowly withering away, and only one, two, or three steps removed from ghost-town status. It is difficult to explain the melancholy I associate with these little places, but never-ending questions always accompany such bleak townscapes. Why did people settle here and then leave? What are the stories behind the forlorn boarded storefronts? Why are so many homes vacated? There are always mysteries associated with lonely burgs, and too often, insightfulness exits into left field. We tend to observe abandonments as unique happenings. Still, such incidents are far removed from this singleness because nothing exists in a void—more substantial, ominous forces are always at play. An abandonment, even a crumbling community, was once part of something dynamic and served as an interdependent entity. Observing one closed factory or one shuttered retail site in light of the larger economic and environmental scene is vital for understanding the reality of the situation. Once the multi-dimensional picture is studied, one recognizes loss on a grand scale—the dead Main Street, repeating vacant storefronts, blocks of empty homes, shuttered factories—and perceives the once blaring, but now silent and invisible, screams for a saving of the shared soul; because in a collective, a town, a region, all are affected, all suffer. Ghost towns and even economically depressed areas are afflicted by misfortune and broken dreams. Niland is not bereft of such features.

A courageous and hardened few still live by the Salton Sea, with the east shore town of Niland holding some of the remaining brave souls. Niland lost more than half of its population since 2010 and now has a populace of about 500 given the 2020 count. Further, a devastating 2020 wildfire wiped out about ten percent of Niland's homes and forced a large evacuation of residents. This tragedy, coupled with Niland's high unemployment rate and ravages of COVID-19, are additional blows to the struggling community. When one views a satellite map of the Imperial Valley, Niland is a small, fading town at the northern tip of the emerald green agricultural richness to the south. Niland is near the southern end of the Salton Sea and is the closest town and shopping center for anyone living in Bombay Beach, Slab City, and other east shore territories. "Shopping center," though, is a generous term for the slight stretch of Niland that only offers one gas station, the Buckshot Deli and Café (quite good actually), and a windowless grocery store featuring many exterior poster advertisements for beer, including a few commands to "Buy American" beer. The shopping scraps of Niland are what the Salton Sea communities depend on for their living needs. If one wants a greater variety of groceries or other retail offerings, a trek requiring an additional eighteen miles south to Brawley is necessary.

As noted, Niland did not always struggle as much as it does today. In the late nineteenth century, Salton Sea's soil was fertile and the Colorado River irrigation project seated Niland's first identity as Old Beach. The 1904 irrigation project brought forth agricultural settlements within the area. With the Southern Pacific completing its rail line in 1904, Old Beach transformed into Imperial Junction. In 1913, Niland was anointed Hobgood for a short time, named after the area's pioneer, John Hobgood. In 1914, though, the Imperial Farm Lands Association, in search of territory investors, minted Niland's name and its name-play on Africa's lush lands paralleling the Nile River. Of course, the evolution of the Salton Sea story is now familiar, and the region's descent and continuing arc of misery commenced in the last half of the twentieth century. Ironically, Egypt, Ethiopia, and Sudan are squabbling over Nile River rights, and these countries' circumstances are complicated with population growth in cities along the Nile, climate change, water salinity escalation, variable water levels, and increased demand for a decreasing water supply—paralleling California's plight. Outsourced water gave birth to Salton Sink life—population, agriculture, tourism, fishing, flora, and fauna—then never-ending dusty layers of despair emerged because of such water, or lack of it. What happens when we are not responsible stewards of our environment? I hope the photographs in this book reveal the impact of political recklessness, neglect, and waste, and prompt an awakening for a win-win call to action for a Sea remedy.

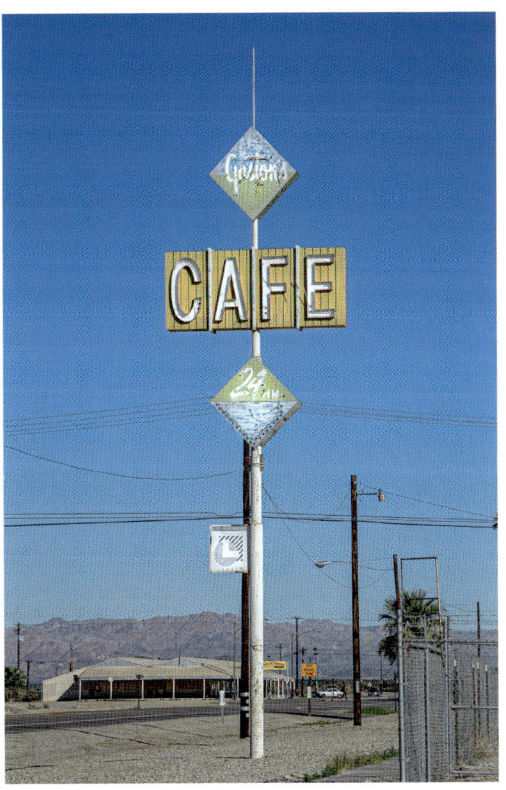

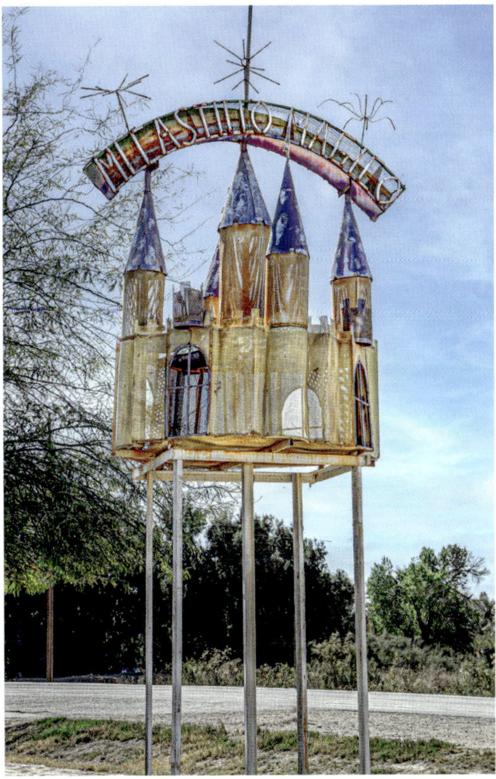

◀ **GASTON'S:** Once a bastion for hunters, fisherman, and truckers on Niland's Highway 111, the only remaining artifact of the once busy Gaston's café is its cast-off sign.

▶ **MI CASTILLO MAGICO:** The sign for the abandoned My Magic Castle still stands in Niland. The site was not magical enough to prevent its closure.

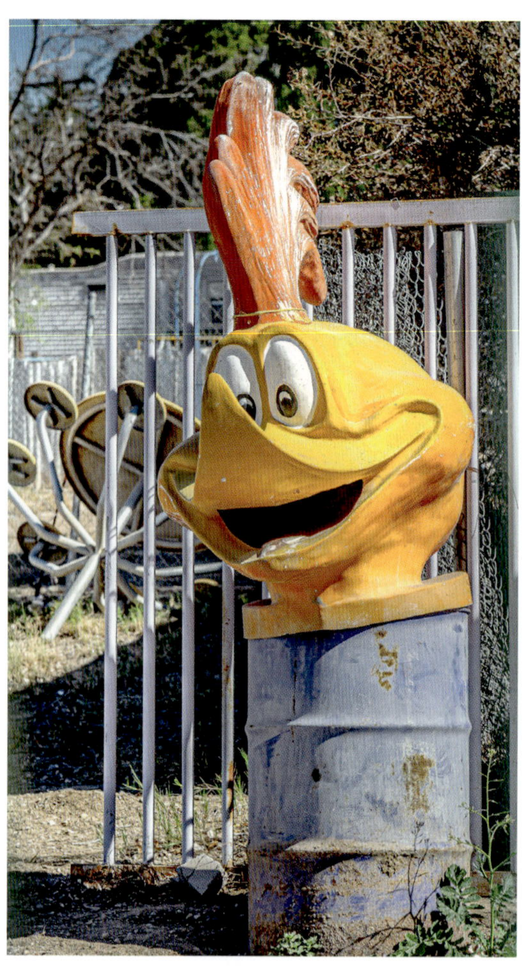

▲ **CLOSED ROADSIDE ATTRACTION:**
A former roadside café once offered cheerful child-friendly features.

▼ **THE SHELL OF AN ABANDONED BUSINESS:**
The percentage of Niland residents living in poverty in 2019 was at 60%.

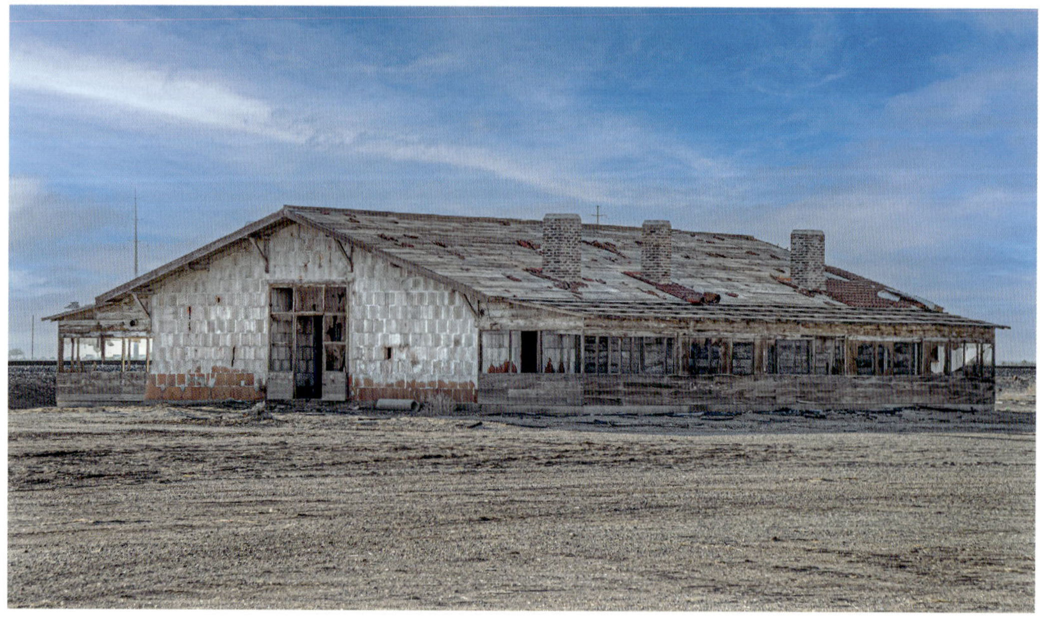

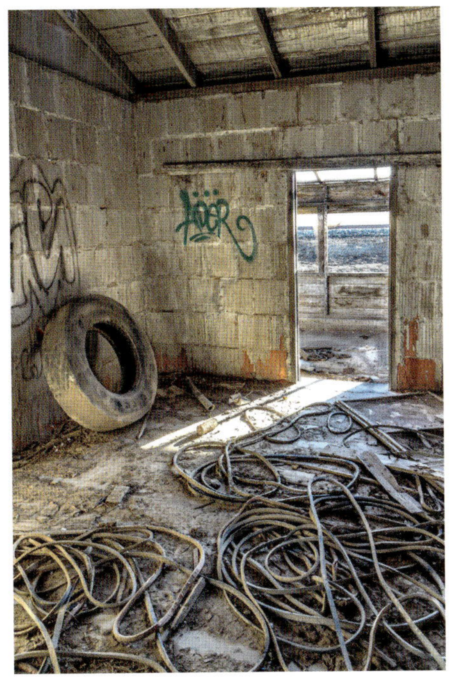

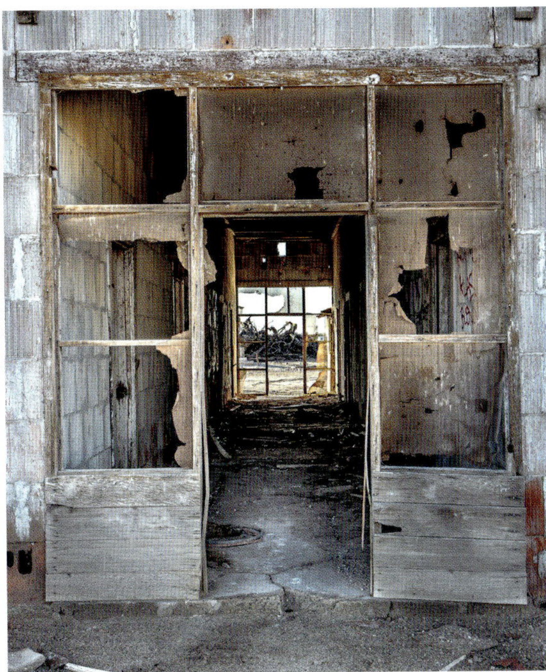

◀ **REMAINS OF A FACTORY:** Niland's population in 2018 was 515 and unable to support a prosperous industrial base.

▶ **ENTRANCE TO ABANDONED FACTORY:** The most common Niland occupations are fishing, farming, and forestry.

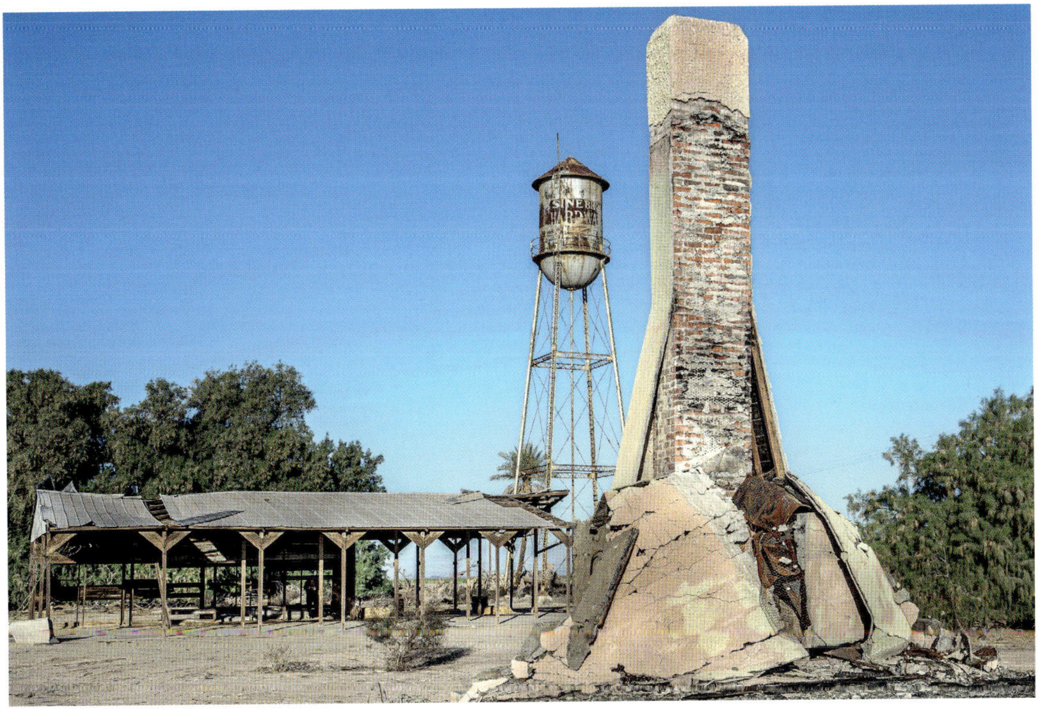

FARM RUINS: While agriculture is still a prime occupation in Niland, the population is too small to support large farming industries.

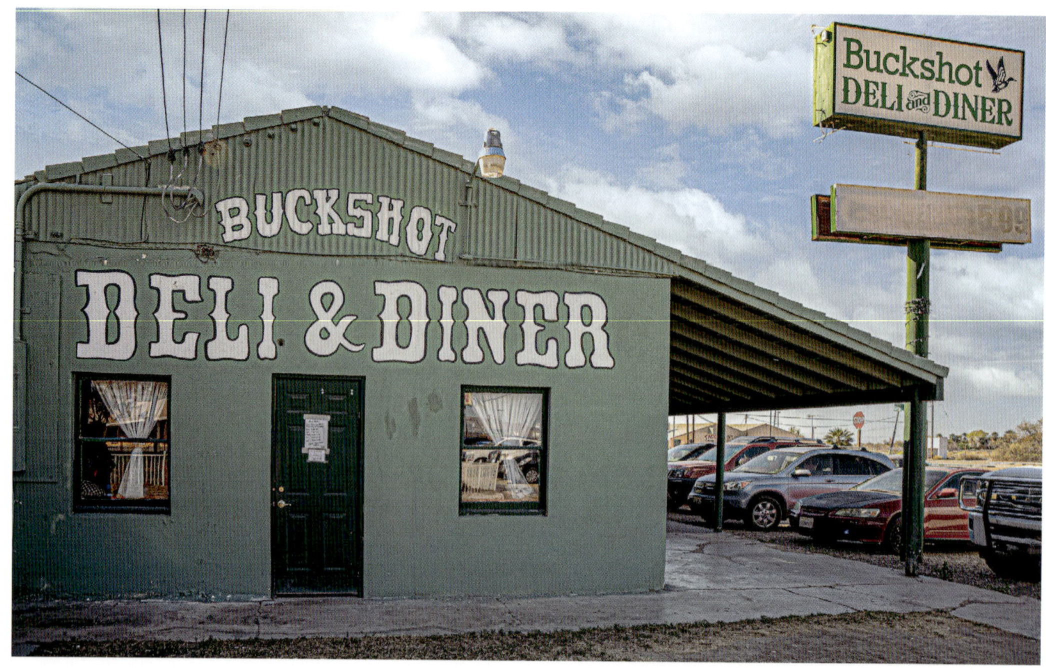

BUCKSHOT DINER: Although not abandoned, Buckshot Diner is one of the few remaining Niland businesses.

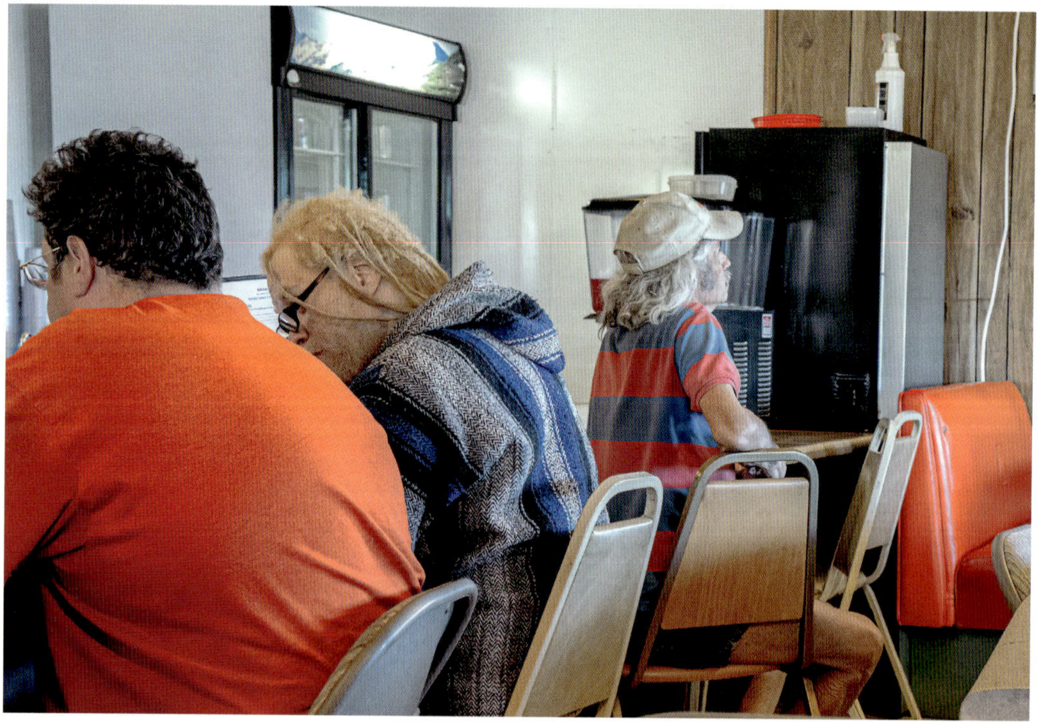

BUCKSHOT BREAKFAST TIME: Buckshot is ranked at the top for best eating establishments in the area.

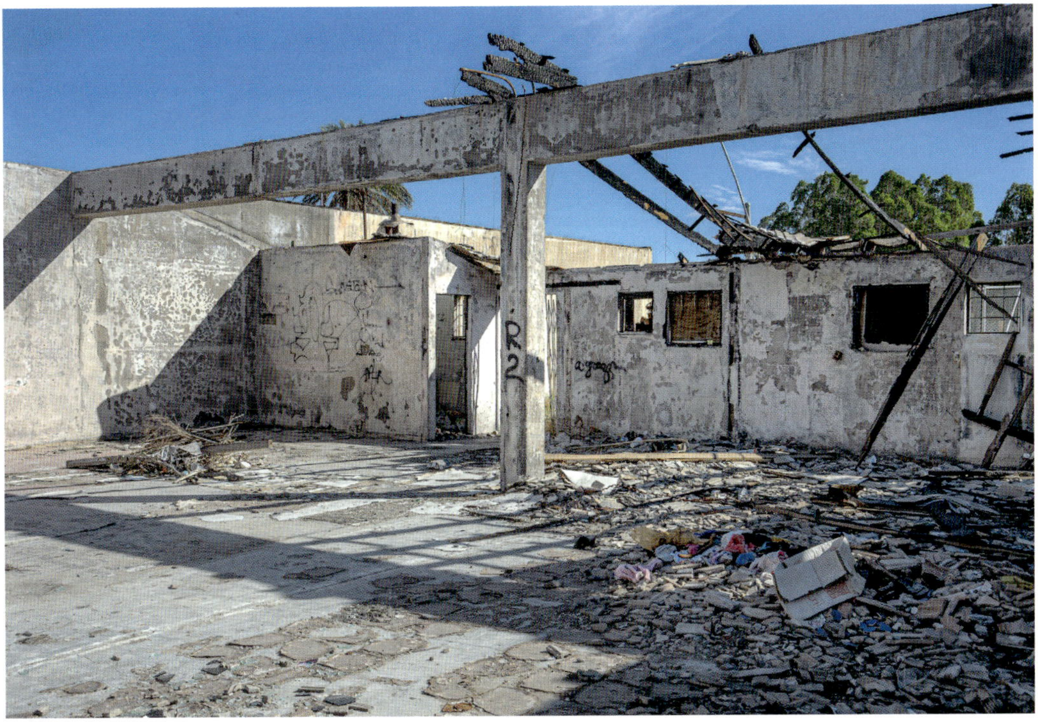

▲ **FIRE DAMAGED RETAIL CENTER:** A small retail strip center is gutted from fire. A Niland local said this was a former tomato processing site, as Niland was once known as the Tomato Capital of the World.

▼ **FISH ART:** Dead fish are even found on the sidewalks and streets of Niland.

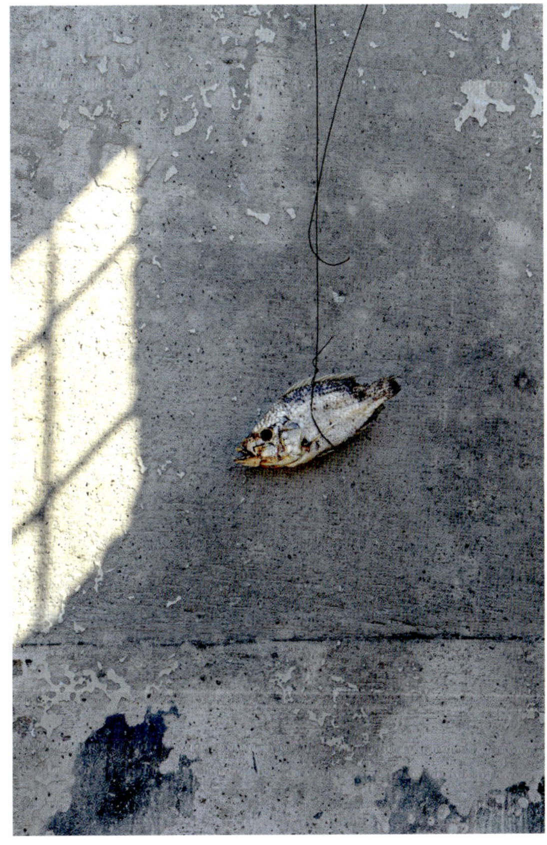

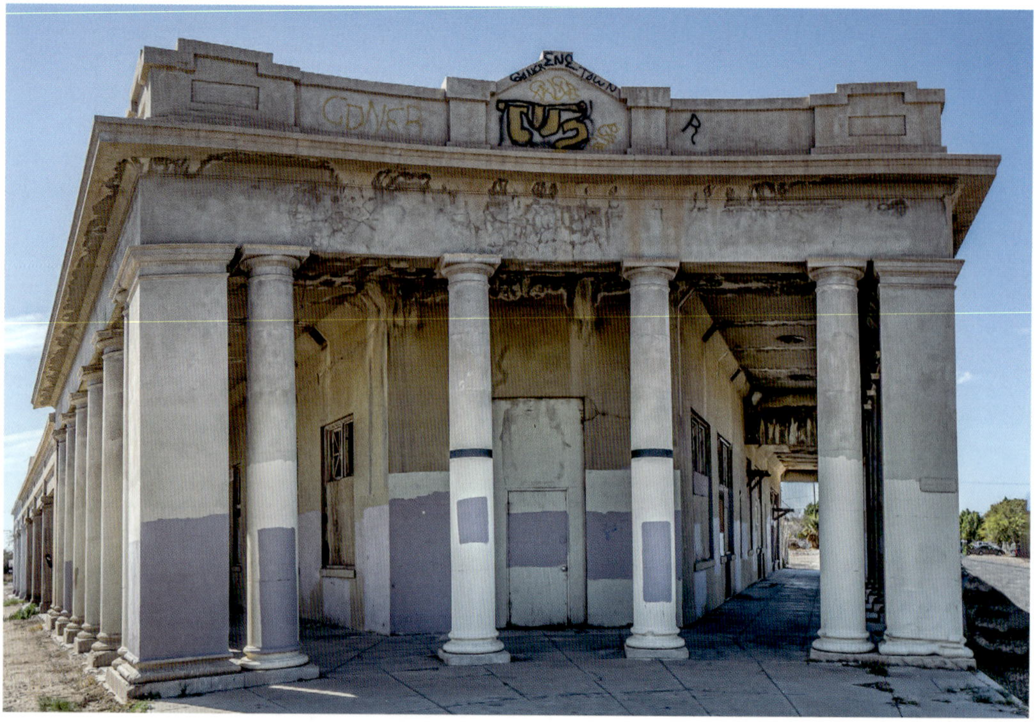

FORMER FIRST NATIONAL BANK AND COMMERCIAL CENTER: Niland is located at the junction of the Imperial Valley and Southern Pacific line. The bank was chartered in 1920 and closed in the early 2000s.

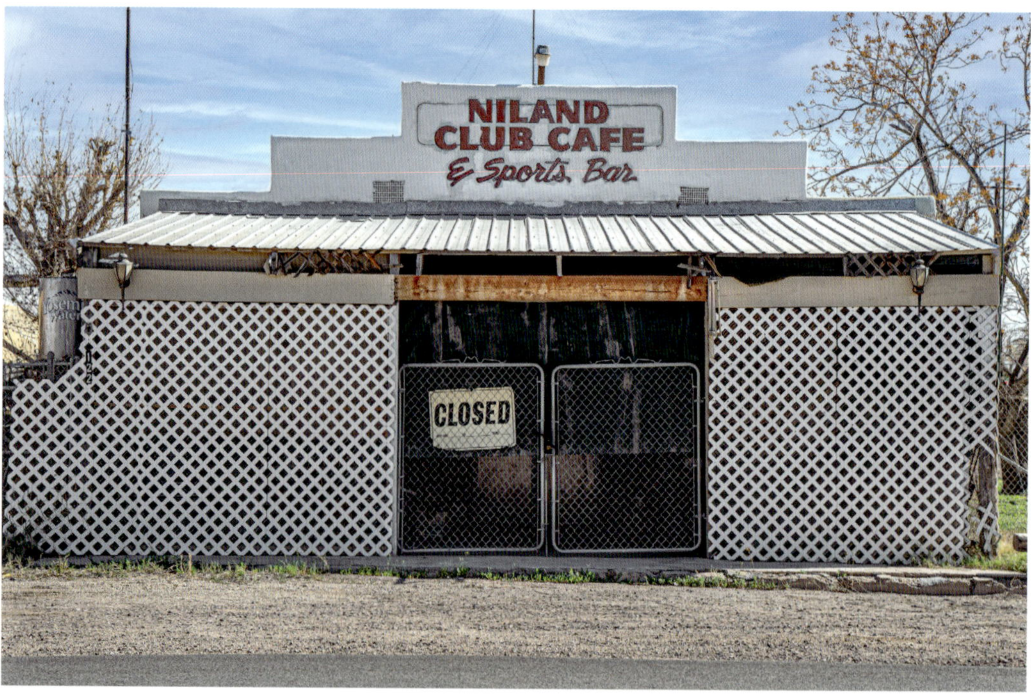

CLOSED CLUB CAFE: With a population exodus decades ago, many small Niland businesses were unable to remain solvent and were forced to close.

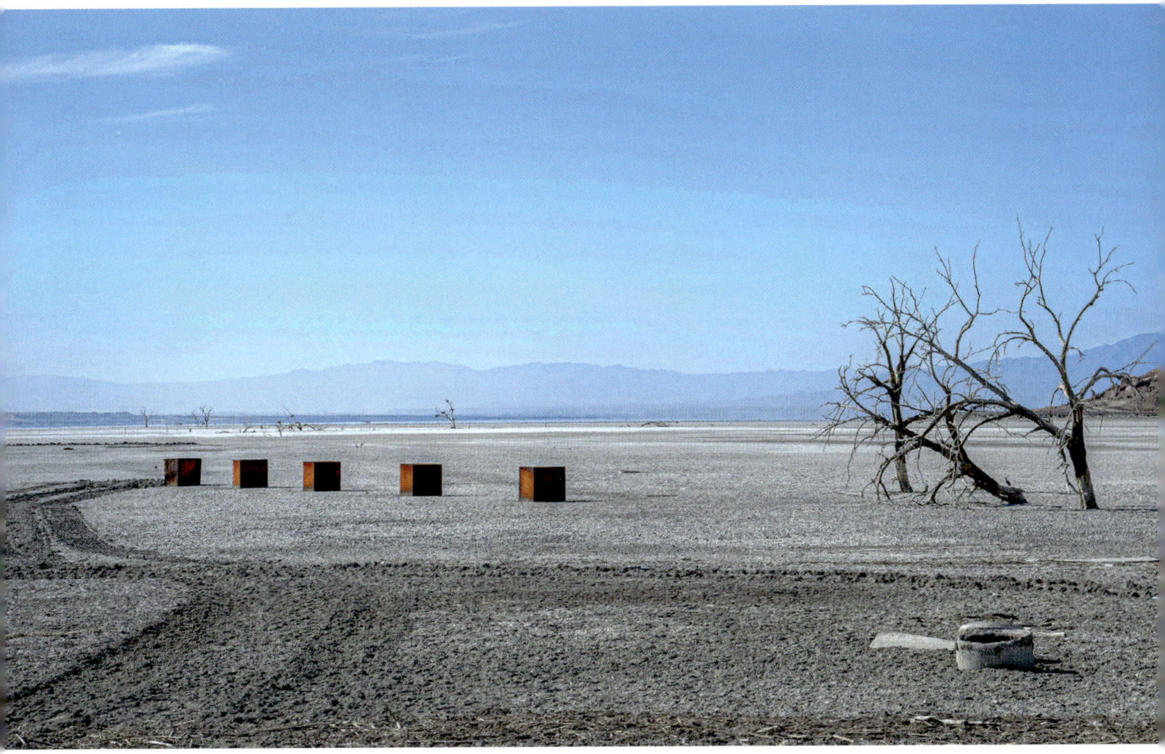

▲ **ART INSTALLATION ON SALTON SEA PLAYA:** Random art installations appear on the playa near Niland, such as this one.

▼ **ALIEN CRASH LANDING?:** This odd roadside art installation is near Niland and Slab City.

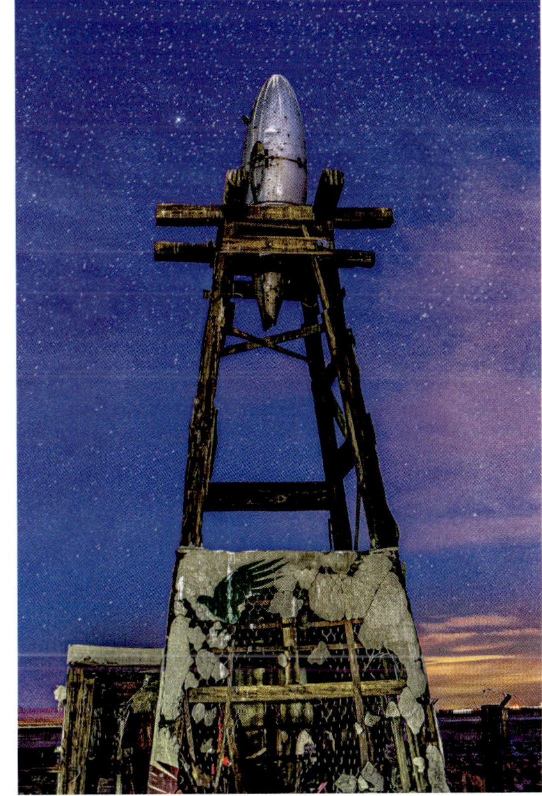

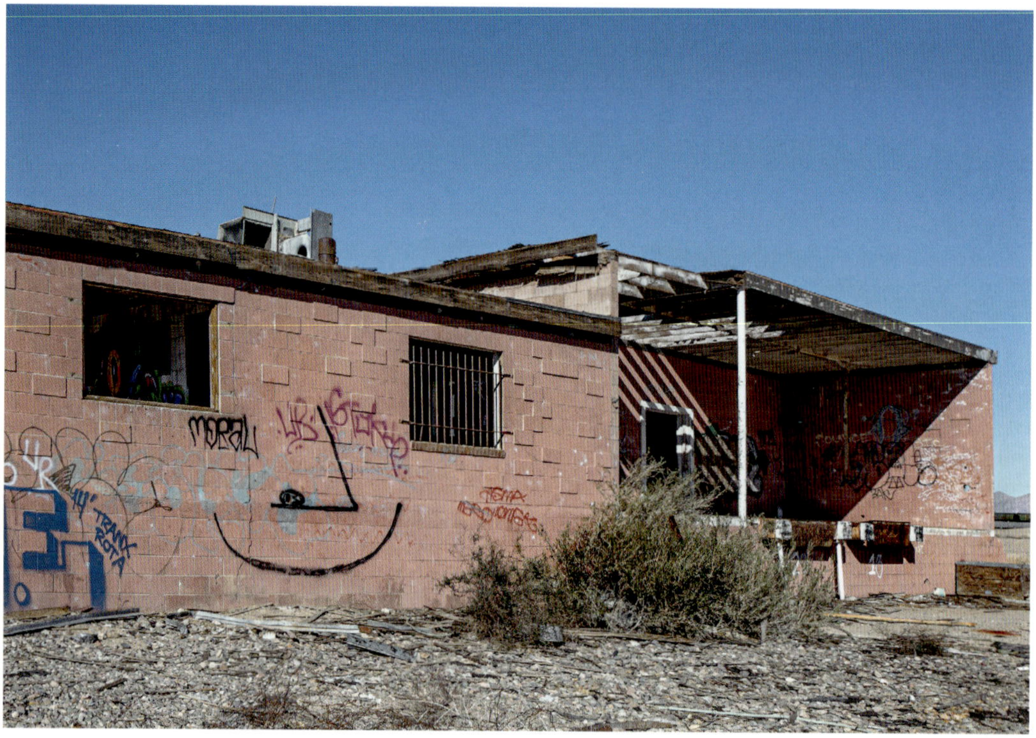

ABANDONED: A Niland local said this forlorn structure was once a busy postal facility.

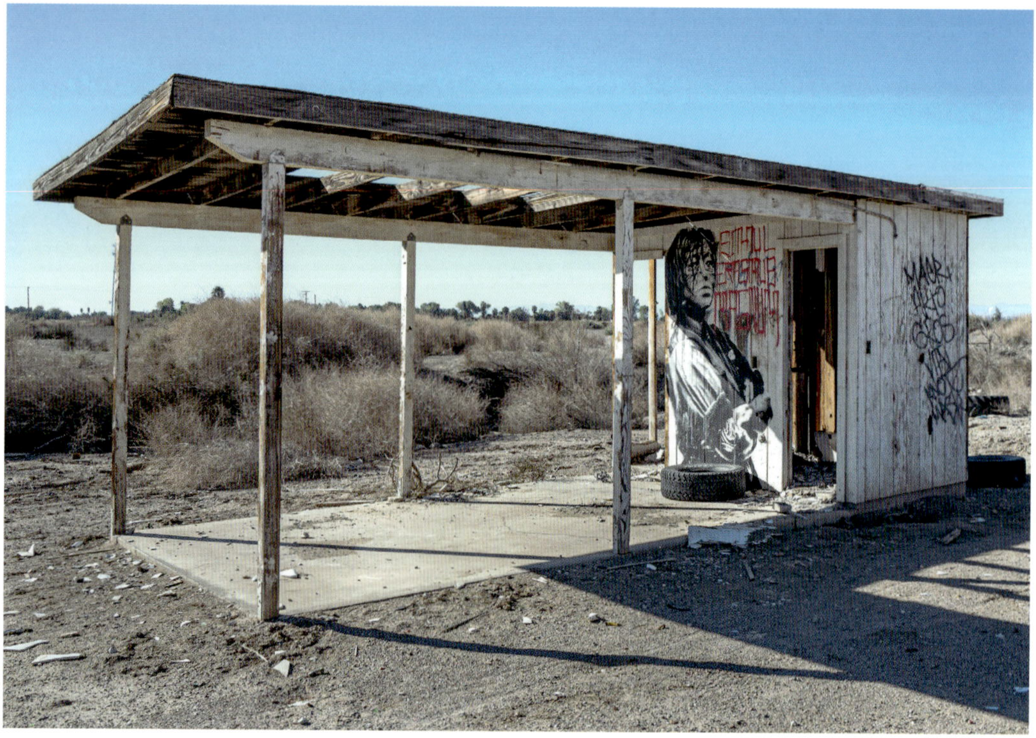

LAST STOP: Is this a bus stop? The last bus departed decades ago and never returned.

7

MONUMENTS TO FOLLY

Praise and blame, gain and loss, pleasure and sorrow come and go like the wind. To be happy, rest like a giant tree in the midst of them all.

Buddha's Little Instruction Book

The dead trees of the Salton Sea stand tall and steady as if they are proud memorials to man's environmental carelessness. I love trees, and we take them for granted and assume they will always be vibrant and plentiful as constant symbols of the greater good. Likewise, trees hold salient positions within the realm of spirituality. Biblical scriptures refer to the Tree of Life, with its growing Garden of Eden tree and the source of eternal life. Buddha realized enlightenment beneath the Bodhi tree. Siddhartha Gautama observed the Druids' venerated rituals among revered stands of trees. Judaism views the Tree of Life as that which braves and feeds life within Yahweh's Garden. Islamic teachings speak of the Tree of Immortality. For centuries, trees are metaphors for life and spiritual growth—stay deeply rooted for worthy life endeavors.

Yes, we assume trees will always be landscape fixtures of beauty and primary actors within noble allegories. Still, too many trees of late are declarations of impending ecological doom and at the mercy of global warming or other manufactured calamities. Countless trees are sickly and roar warning signs about the state of our planet's health. The Salton Sea is a continuous shriek of ecological caution, and its stately dead trees resemble nature's doomed poster children placed against an arid landscape. Nevertheless, I found so many lifeless trees as beauteous, especially when silhouetted against the spectacular Sea-colored sunsets and sunrises. There is unadorned beauty with a dead tree, too—the gnarled texture of the dried wood and the sinuous contours of bleached branches. Dead trees, often referred to as snags, are indispensable sources of shelter, food, and rest stops for the Sea's remaining wildlife. I loved seeing the Cormorants perched on dead branches for their chatty sunset happy hours and outlined against a sky of cobalt and ginger luminosity. Symbolically too, there is the life that joins with death. The birds represent life and freedom, while the snag presents the end—death. Because so many birds use the lifeless trees for nesting and perching, an interdependent relationship forms and emblematically—life and death are closer to each other than perceived. Always captivating, the simple beauty of the Sea snags merit memorable songs of praise, with their magnificent legacy still strongly echoing across the desert panorama.

The curves of snags present bold contrasts against flaming radioactive-esque sunrises or soft water-colored pastel sunsets. Each sunset and sunrise of the Sea forces one to pause and absorb the stunning movement and color on a rapidly evolving frame showcasing the grandeur of the black silhouetted snags. No two sunsets or sunrises are ever the same and are fitting milieus to distinguish the once resplendent life of a grand tree. Trees sit in one spot for decades and are silent witnesses to all change that passes by. After a good life, a tree's essence remains, and even if it is devoid of life, its presence forces contemplation—lessons abound. Dead trees can represent, however, the calling for rebirth. Like many life lessons, traveling through blackness must be experienced before the lightness appears and is appreciated. The Sea is still embroiled in a lengthy road of great darkness and is overdue for light and renewal—an unmistakable message as one contemplates a lone snag on the Sea playa.

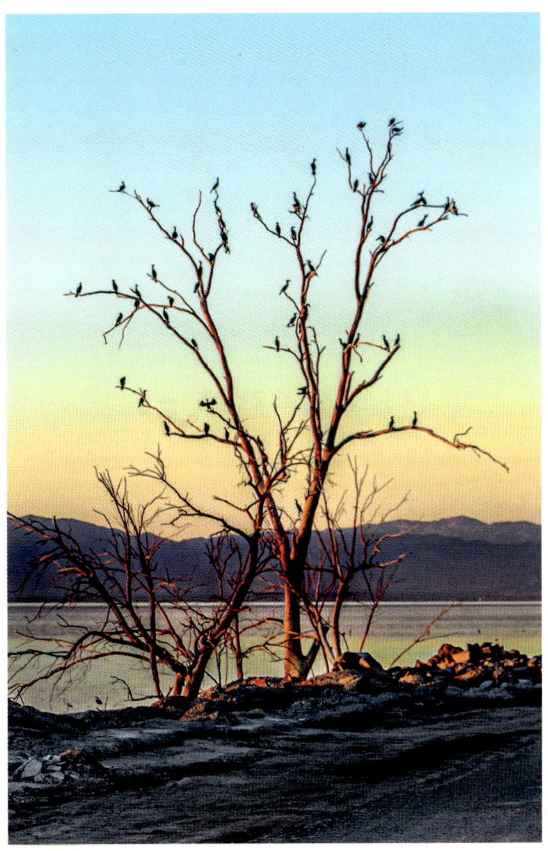

▲ **SUNSET CORMORANT GATHERING:** "Every sunset brings the promise of a new dawn." Ralph Waldo Emerson

▼ **LANDSCAPE AT SUNSET:** Every sunset presents a gift to recharge for the coming day.

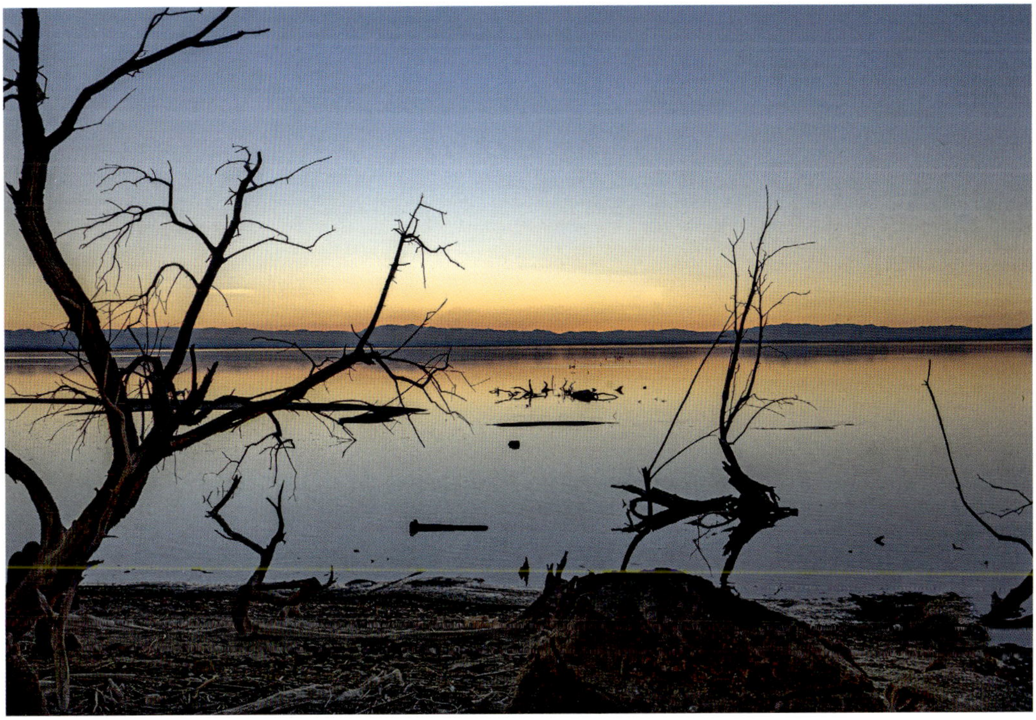

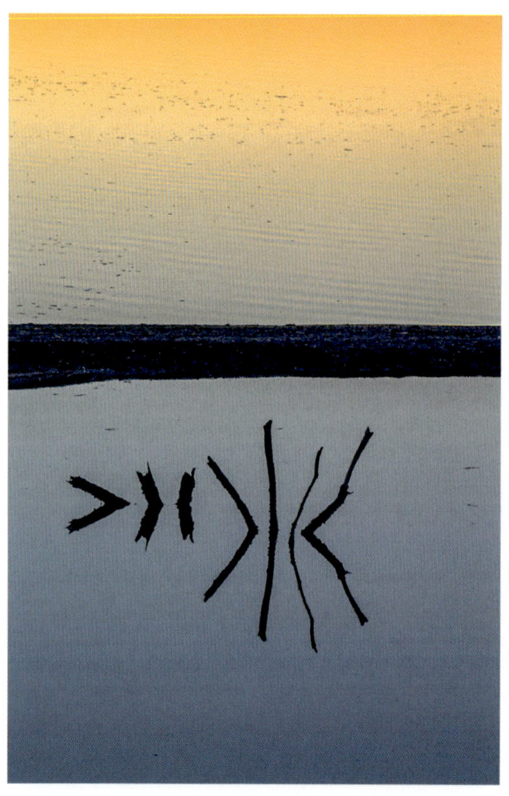

ARTFUL SUNSET: Stark and simple reflective beauty.

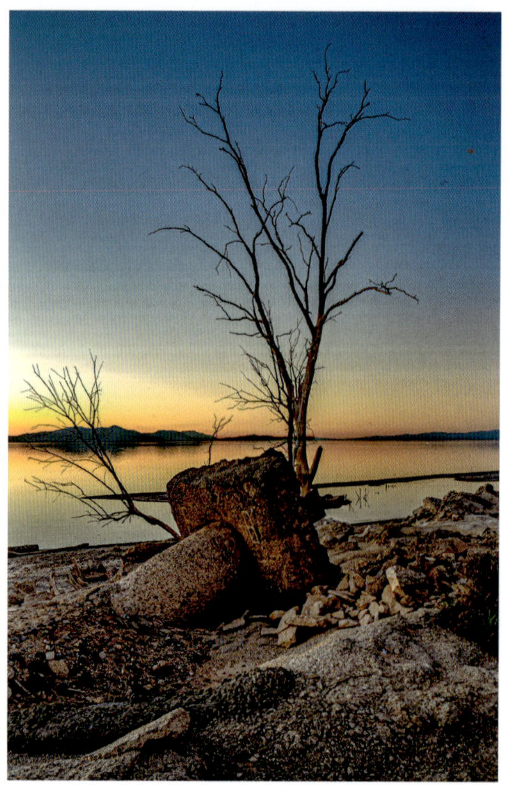

ORGANIC AND INDUSTRIAL REMAINS: The barren earth and blight of the Salton Sea reveal the dead trees, but the spectacular sunsets allow for striking tree silhouettes against a vividly colored sky.

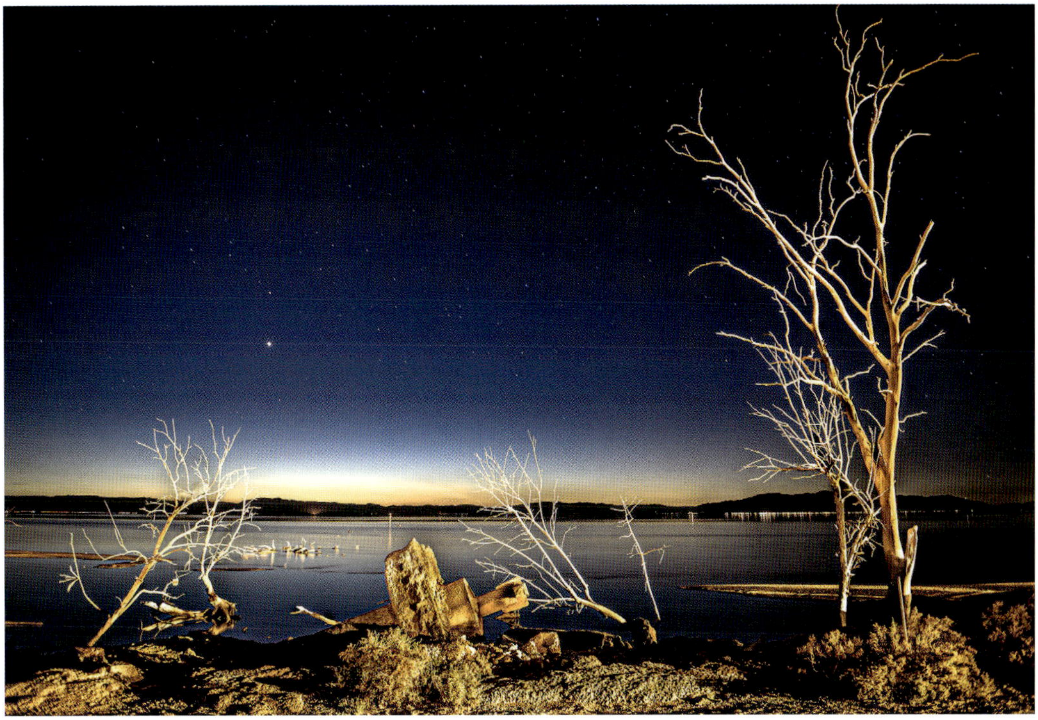

BLUE HOUR: The nearby geo-thermal power plant casts an ethereal and golden glow on the Salton Sea landscape during blue hour.

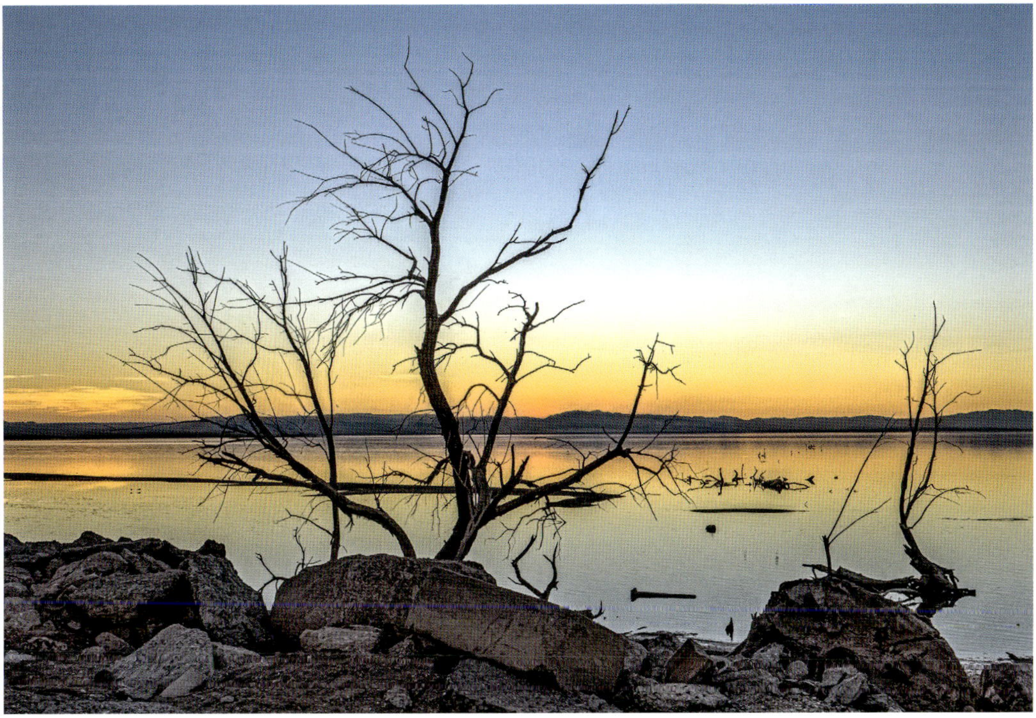

SUNSET: The winter months in the Salton Sea paint the sunset sky in glorious color.

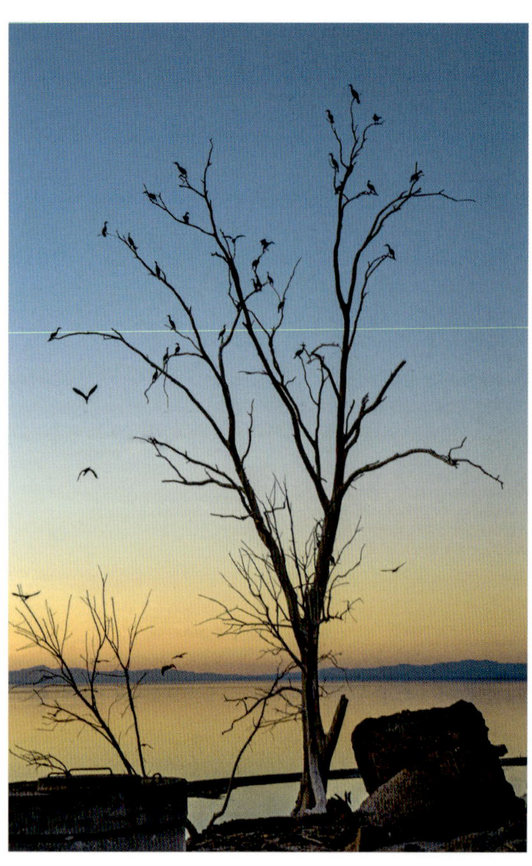

▲ **CORMORANTS PERCHING AT SUNSET:** One needs to pause at sunset and take in its delicate and spectacular movement of color.

▼ **SUNSET LANDSCAPE:** Sunrises and sunsets happen every day, and they are free for the taking.

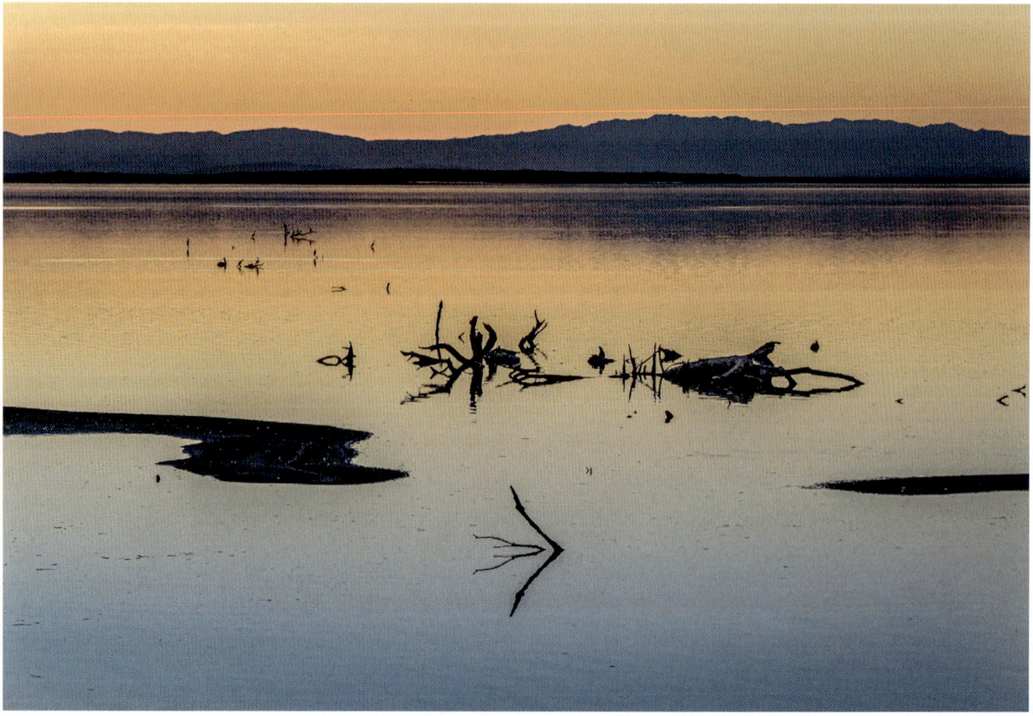

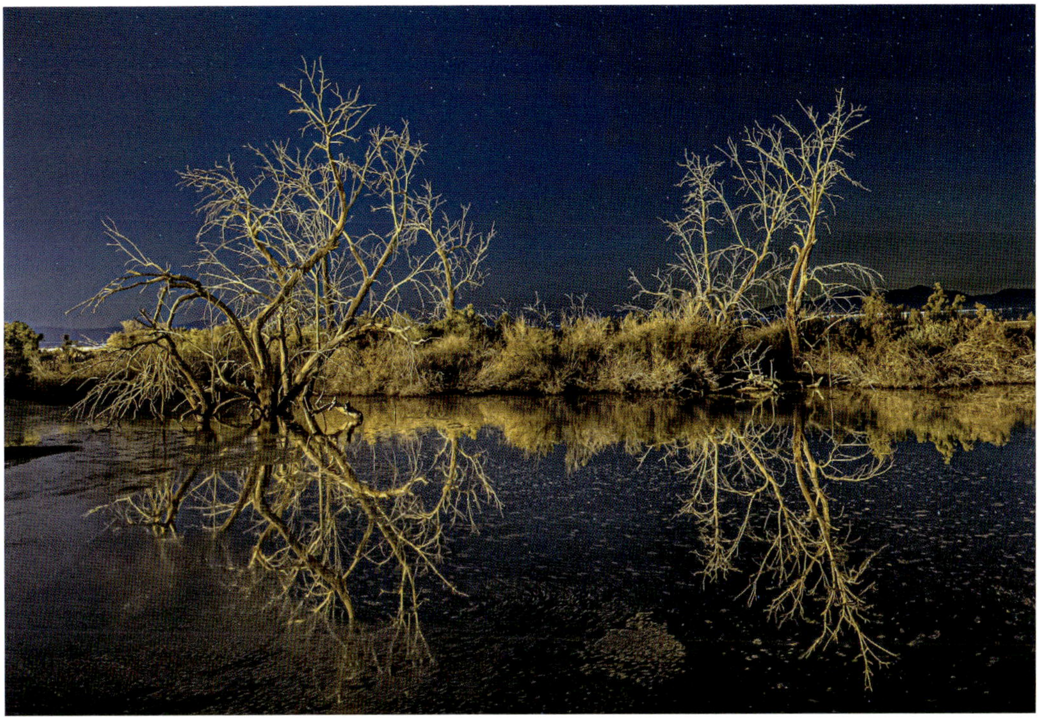

BLUE HOUR REFLECTIONS: The landscape's faint golden glow from the nearby geo-thermal power plant is assisted with some light-painting to pull out the detail and water reflections.

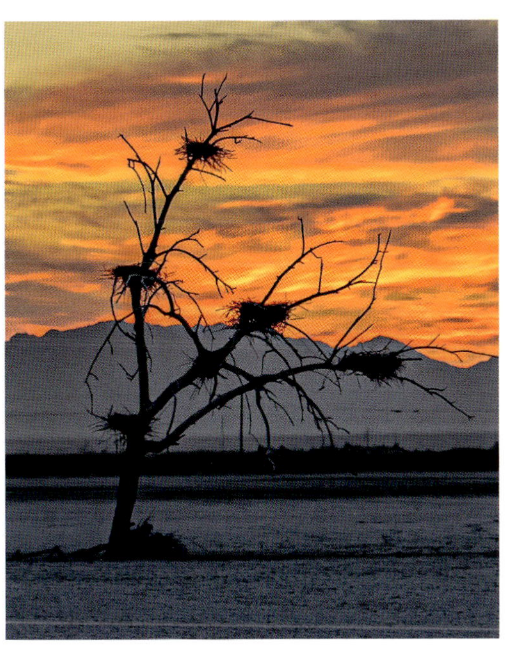

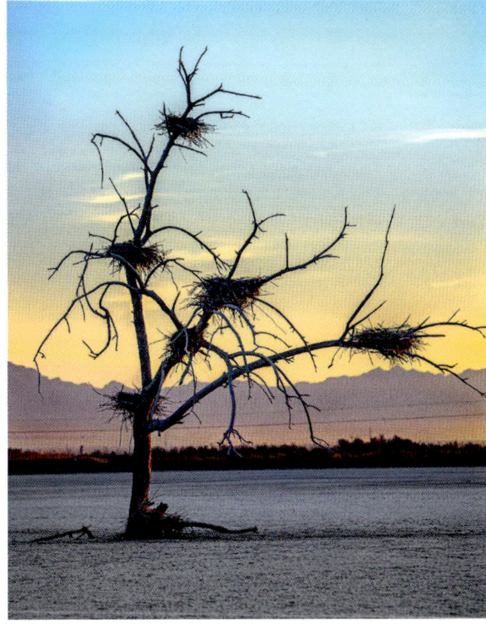

◀ **RED HILL SUNRISE:** Herons' nests pepper the dead tree on the dry Salton Sea playa against a blazing background.

▶ **JUST AFTER SUNRISE ON THE RED HILL PLAYA:** The emerging light of daytime bathes the landscape with evolving color.

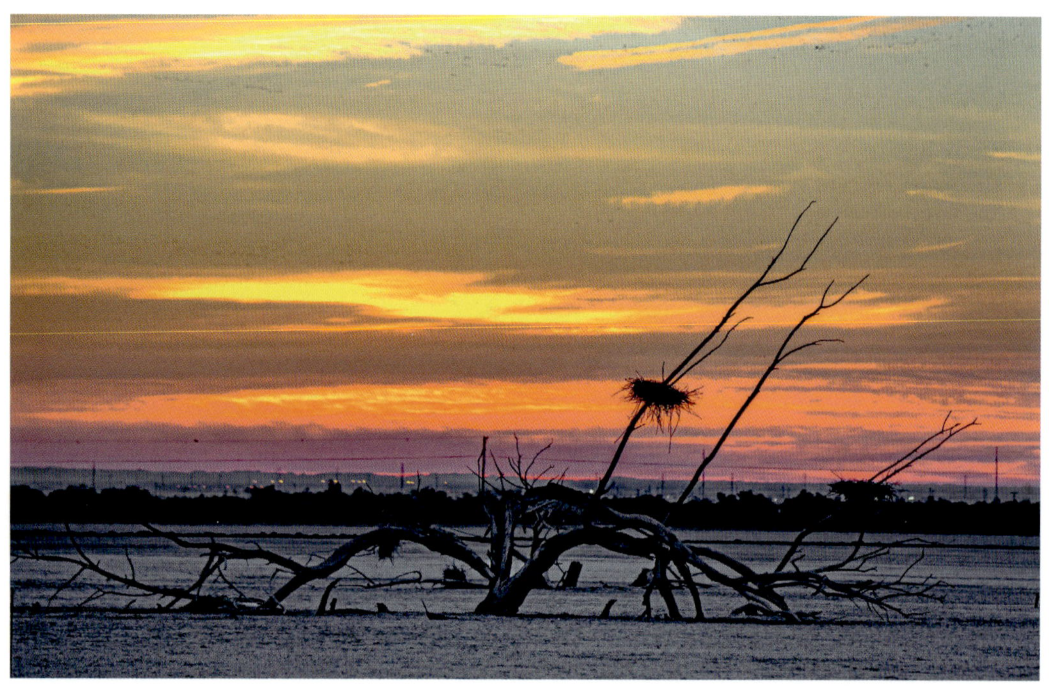

PLAYA SUNRISE: Salton Sea winters grace the sky with glorious purples and oranges as a canvas for a snag silhouette.

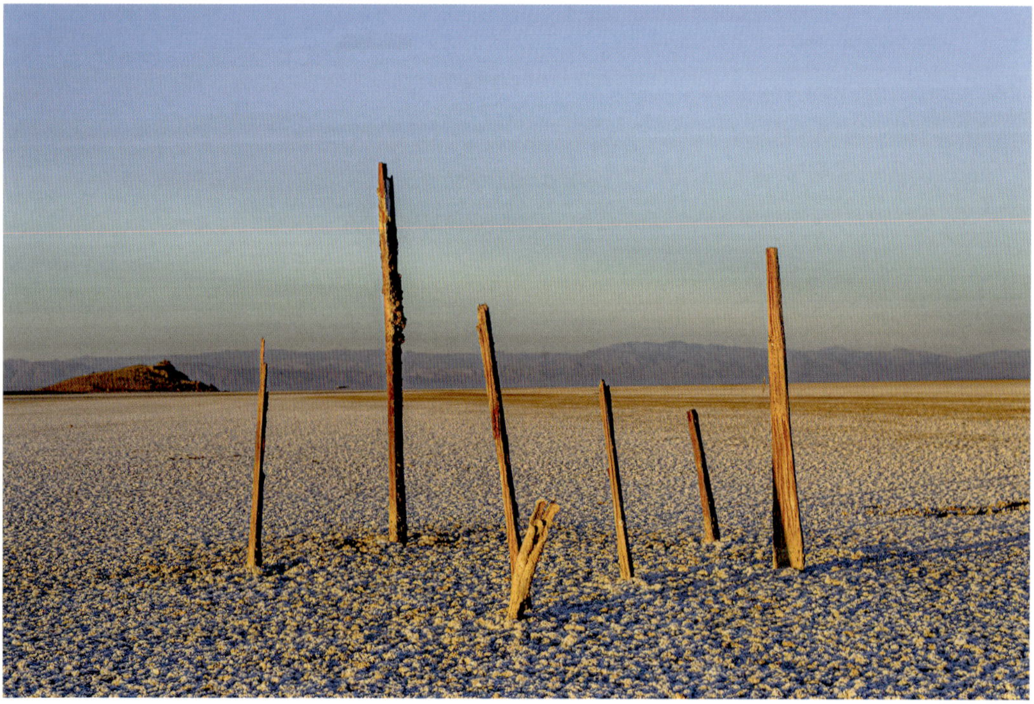

ONCE MAJESTIC TREES: Still beautiful, the stark trunks of the snags stand as strong markers for man's environmental folly.

EPILOGUE:
THE LINE IN THE SAND

> Never doubt that a small group of thoughtful, committed citizens can change the world; indeed, it is the only thing that ever has.
>
> Margaret Mead

California is blessed with endless scenic beauty and plentiful sunshine. The Salton Sea was once a card-carrying member of the California picturesque seascape club. By the 1970s, all but the most hardened residents left the Sea region, and today's communities dotting the coast resemble ghost towns. The Sea is toxic and continues to grow deadlier with each passing year.

The Sea is a looming environmental and public health catastrophe. The Sea's shoreline continues to recede with more and more exposure of the dusty playa. The lakebed holds a century's worth of agricultural run-off, including carcinogenic herbicides. The lakebed toxins take flight and journey into a wide swath of the southwestern United States and Mexico. Alarms about this precarious situation have been blaring for decades.

California is primarily responsible for the Sea's mitigation since 2017. The Imperial Irrigation District supplied water to the Sea since 2003 per the Quantification Settlement Agreement between Colorado River patrons and Southern California water districts. The Imperial Irrigation District agreed to prevent the Sea from evaporating by mining water saved through various conservation measures. Still, this agreement was only a temporary measure, and aquatic inflows to the Sea ceased in 2017 with California assuming Sea management. In 2017, some projects for restoration commenced and included the creation of ponds and ditches around the Sea for the cultivation of fish habitats and abatement of airborne dust. One major challenge remains—tapping a new source of freshwater for stable water salinity. Several proposals are on the development table and include the import and desalination of ocean water via a pipeline and the supplementation with agricultural return flows or water run-off from irrigated farmlands. The goal of the Salton Sea Management Program, nevertheless, is to create wetlands surrounding the Sea but also, perhaps, the maintenance of a lesser but restored lake.

In 2019, California's Governor Gavin Newsom and Secretary of Natural Resources, Wade Crowfoot, pledged to resolve the matters dogging the Sea. Action must follow promises, of course, and Newsom and Crowfoot must ensure that the Salton Sea Management Program installs a team of qualified individuals to safeguard the projects. California must improve its liaison with the representatives and business leaders of Riverside and Imperial Counties—often neglected, underrepresented, and ignored. California implemented a scheme to jacket 4,000 acres of exposed lakebed with shallow water. However, such a project is stymied by the reality that the Colorado River basin is suffering a two-decade drought, with perhaps the driest period in more than 1,000 years according to fossil data. Indeed, many regions of the United States are suffering a significant and extended drought. Less water flowing downriver from the Colorado is also problematic for the drinking water supply serving the expanding urban areas along the river. Accordingly, California's officials are under mounting pressure to lessen the Sea's impact with a concurring escalating health crisis.

Additionally, the U.S. Southwest is developing so fast and in need of fresh water. Because the cities along the Colorado River are expanding too, perhaps the only reasonable solution for a healthy Sea appears to rest on the conveyance of ocean water. In contrast to California mitigation proposals, this recommendation is featured in the Save Our Sea Campaign, and at face value, appears to be a reasonable fix. Is this a pipe dream or a genuine solution? It is not unrealistic to construct a pipeline or canal from the Gulf of California to the Sea. Water can flow by gravity because the Sea rests more than 200 feet below sea level. A conduit with a series of locks for gravity-controlled water flow seems to be a workable solution. Further, Laguna Salada from the Sea of Cortez in Mexico is only about 15-20 miles from the Sea and allows for a descending gravity water flow—a very feasible option. Similarly, the Middle East is undertaking such a project from the Red Sea to the Dead Sea, called the Two-Seas Canal. Options for Salton Sea water desalinization are at hand, too. The geothermal resources to power desalination via renewable resources are at the ready in the Sea region with its ten geothermal plants. Moreover, clean water for the Sea would be available for the U.S. Southwest region with this plan. The multiple benefits inherent within the Save our Sea Campaign are attractive. The costs involved are much less compared to the outlays of other California grand-scale mollification programs. In essence, the Save Our Sea Campaign can import water from the ocean, cover the dust, desalinate the water, and provide clean water for many. Ultimately, this plan's successful implementation might promote the return of population to the Sea region, and as a bonus, improve relations between the U.S. and Mexico. However, restoring the Sea would most likely be the most significant North American water effort since the 1930s Hoover Dam project; indisputably, a daunting task. Still, I fear with the U.S. held hostage within the grips of a fierce drought, any attention to Sea palliation might evolve into a murky vision.

On October 22, 2019, Imperial County and its board of supervisors unanimously voted to declare a state of local emergency due to the Sea air pollution. Also, the California Natural Resources Agency was directed to produce a long-term Sea fix by the end of 2022. Although eleven plans are under Agency review, the most feasible scheme appears to be the transfer of water across the U.S.-Mexico border from the Sea of Cortez to the Salton Sea. The grim reality is here, but does anyone care beyond the Sea? The ecological Sea time-bomb is ticking and will soon cross the rubicon of health crises for an area that will extend far beyond the Sea region and carry cascading fiscal and health costs for the region and country. The Sea teeters between purgatory and hell and is hoarse from decades of shouts for salvation—a forgotten place. With climate change on the nation's political agenda, is the Sea just a microcosm of our shared environmental future? The Salton Sea presents the death of the American dream, and on so many literal and figurative levels, is as fetid as its bone beaches. Humanity altered the natural Sea landscape, and logic dictates that humanity now has a duty to manage and heal its unnatural handiwork; but, is it too late for a save? Have we reached the line in the Salton Sea sand?

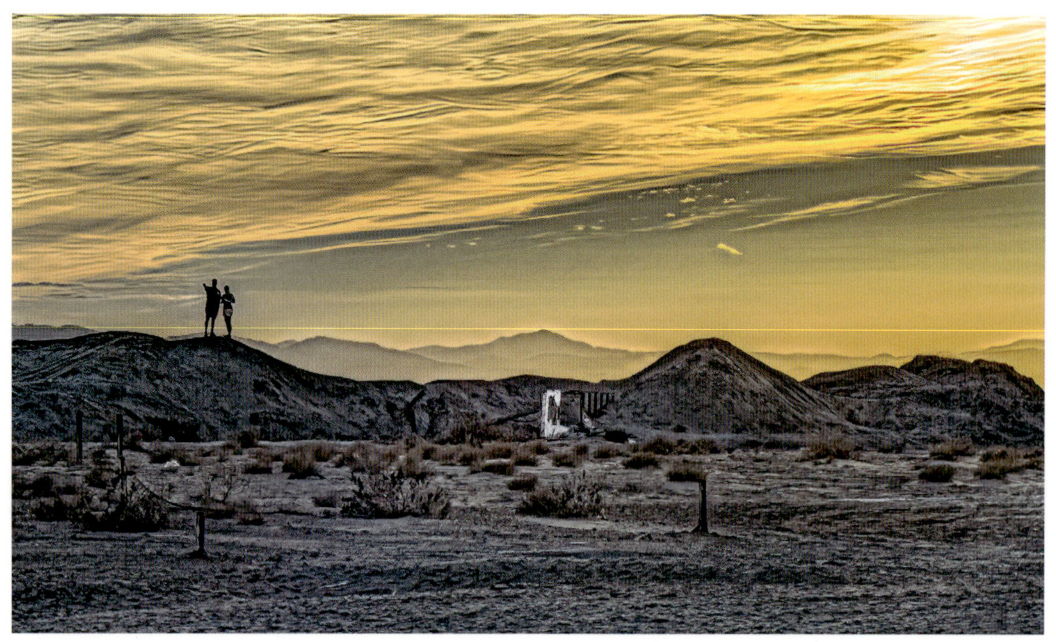

BOMBAY BEACH: A few souls pondering the Bombay Beach landscape at dusk. What is its future?

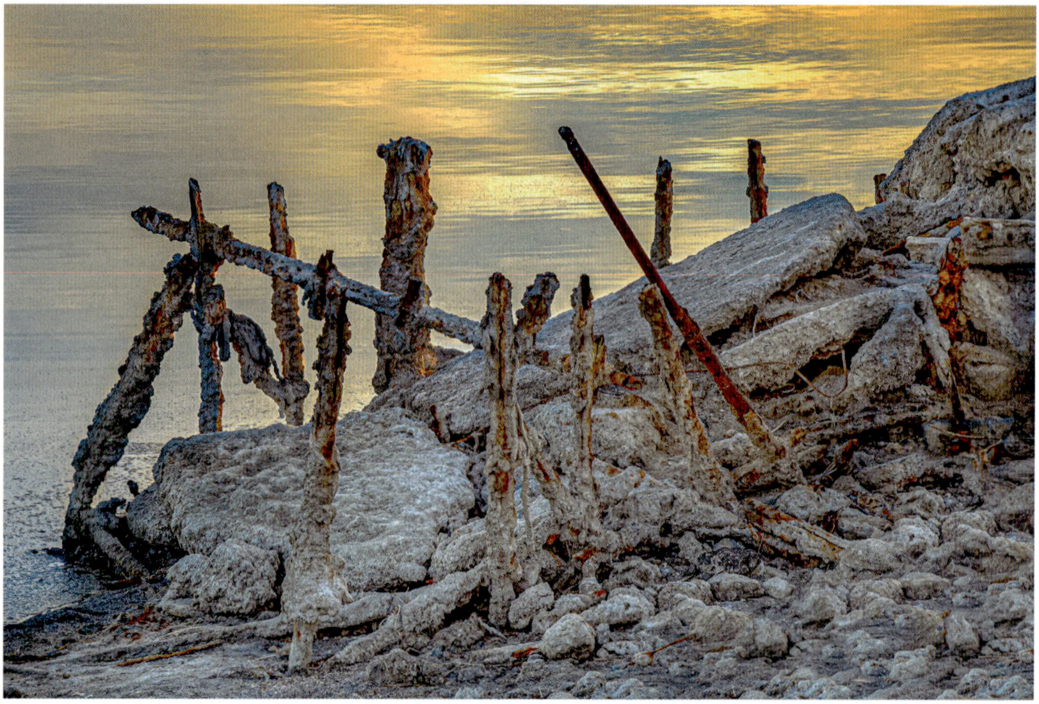

BOMBAY BEACH: The detritus of man-made recklessness.

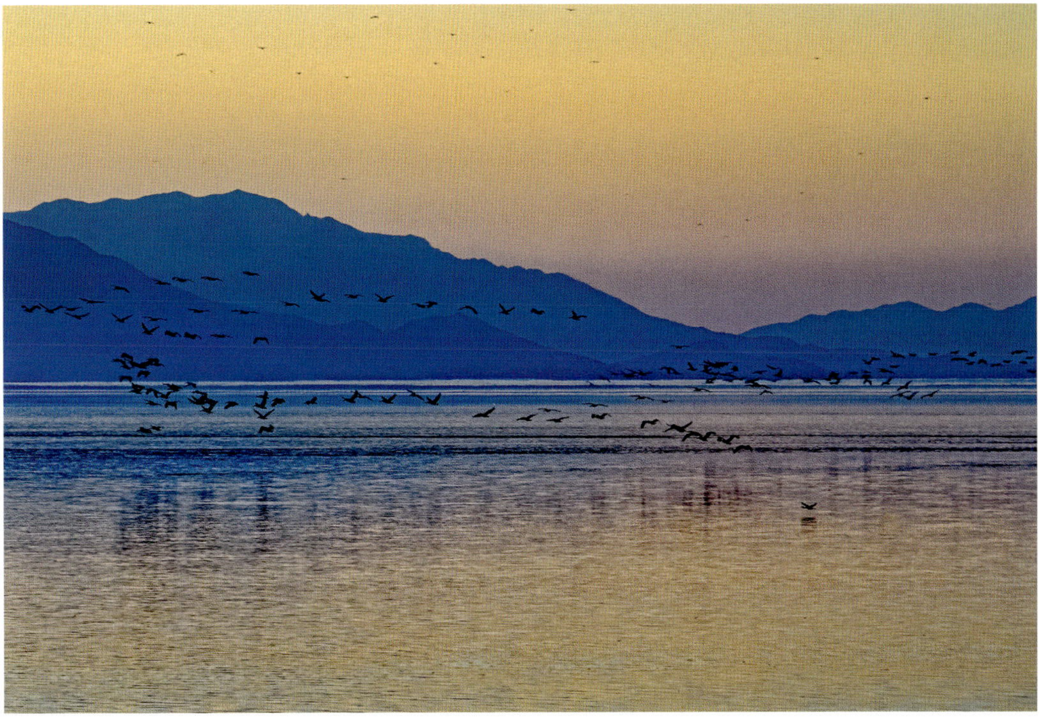

EAST SHORE SUNSET SILHOUETTE: Nature still delivers gifts at sundown and veils the environmental damage of man's reckless hand.

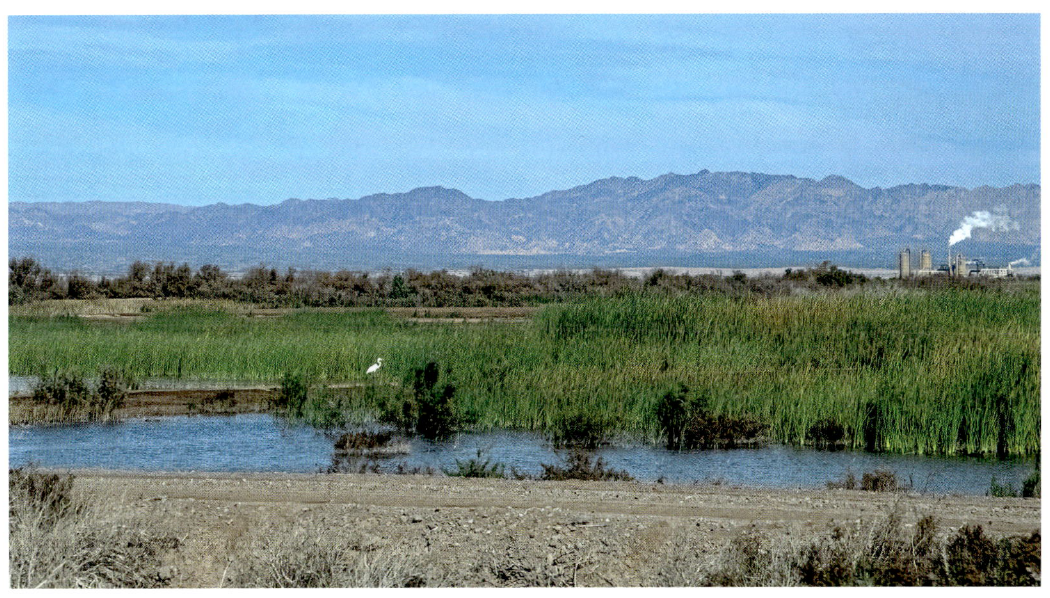

IMPERIAL VALLEY IRRIGATION CANALS, EGRET AND GEO-THERMAL PLANT: The ecological point of no return for the Salton Sea is imminent without needed intelligent governmental insight and planning.

BIBLIOGRAPHY

Anderson, Ian. "How Bombay Beach Has Gone from Apocalyptic Desert Wasteland to Offbeat Art Hub." Roadtrippers. 11 Feb. 2020. roadtrippers.com/magazine/bombay-beach-apocalyptic-wasteland-art-hub

Anhie. "Slab City." Atlas Obscura. Atlas Obscura, 24 June 2012. atlasobscura.com/places/slab-city-california.

The Atomic Redhead, Janey. "The Deserted Town of Desert Shores." Blog post. Atomic Redhead. atomicredhead.com/2015/03/25/desert-shores/.

Beard, Stephen J., Shawn J. Sullivan, Mark Olalde, and Javier Zarracina. "How to Save the Salton Sea: Proposal to Import Seawater Across California Desert Is Biggest Since Hoover Dam." *USA Today*. Gannett Satellite Information Network, 11 June 2021. usatoday.com/in-depth/graphics/2021/06/11/salton-sea-drying-up-infrastructure-projects/5243837001/.

Bell, Diane. "Column: Unimaginable Tragedy Hits Tiny Imperial County Town." *San Diego Union-Tribune*, 02 July 2020. sandiegouniontribune.com/columnists/story/2020-07-01/column-unimaginable-tragedy-hits-small-imperial-county-town.

C., Farr Ed Finis. *History of Imperial County, California*. Hardpress, 2012. Print.

Cooper, Daniel S. "Protecting Critical Bird Habitat Should Be a Priority at the Salton Sea." July 2016. resources.ca.gov/CNRALegacyFiles/wp-content/uploads/2015/10/Protecting-Birds-at-the-Salton-Sea-Audubon-California.pdf.

DesertUSA.com. "The Kinetoscope and More." DesertUSA. 2018. desertusa.com/desert-people/christina-angelina.

DBPedia.com "About: Salton City, California." DPpedia, 2021. dbpedia.org/page/Salton_City,_California.

Documentary: *Miracle in the Desert Film*. Dir. Greg Bassenian. Salton Sea Documentary. 2020. miracleinthedesert.com.

Frost, Garrison. “Salton Sea’s Iconic Pelicans and Cormorants Are Quickly Becoming a Thing of the Past.” Audubon California. 25 Apr. 2019. ca.audubon.org/press-release/salton-sea%E2%80%99s-iconic-pelicans-and-cormorants-are-quickly-becoming-thing-past.

Goodyear, Dana. “The Dying Sea.” *New Yorker*. 27 Apr. 2015. Print.

Graham, Regina F. “A Ghost Town in the Making: How the Salton Sea Went from Busy Resorts to a ‘Public Health Disaster’.” *Daily Mail Online*. Associated Newspapers, 13 June 2018. dailymail.co.uk/news/article-5839677/A-ghost-town-making-Salton-Sea-went-busy-resorts-public-health-disaster.

Iannamico, Landon Sage, and Sage Alexander. “Weekender: The Salton Sea: The Worst Lake You’ve Never Heard of.” *The Daily Californian*. 09 May 2021. dailycal.org/2021/05/09/the-salton-sea-the-worst-lake-youve-never-heard-of.

Iovenko, Chris. “California’s Largest Lake Is Now a Public-Health Threat.” *The Atlantic*. Atlantic Media Company, 09 Nov. 2015. theatlantic.com/science/archive/2015/11/the-airborne-toxic-lake-event/414888.

Koeppel, Elliot. “Salton Sea - Bombay Beach.” Cali49. 20 June 2015. cali49.com/mojave/2015/3/24/salton-sea-bombay-beach.

Koeppel, Elliot. “Salton Sea - Desert Shores.” Cali49. 24 Oct. 2015. cali49.com/mojave/2015/6/12/salton-sea-desert-shores.

Lavelle, Matthew. “Slab City Is An Off-Grid Desert City, And Its Residents Claim It’s The Last Free Place In America.” Ranker. 19 May 2020. ranker.com/list/facts-about-slab-city/matthew-lavelle.

Levy, Rom. “Fin DAC X Angelina Christina “Shesha Sand Storm” New Street Art - Desert Shores, California.” Street Art News. 07 Nov. 2013. streetartnews.net/2013/11/street-art-findac-angelinachristina-desertshores.

Llamas, Ryan. “What’s Wrong with the Salton Sea?” Audubon California. 04 June 2021. ca.audubon.org/news/whats-wrong-salton-sea.

Lubell, Sam. “Exploring Modern Ruins in Southern California” *New York Times*. 03 Mar. 2019. nytimes.com/2014/03/23/travel/exploring-modern-ruins-in-southern-california.

Murphy, Mary. “East Jesus—the Art in Trash.” Any Excuse to Travel. 05 Mar. 2019. anyexcusetotravel.com/travel/east-jesus-the-art-in-trash.

Nijhuis, Michelle. “Accidental Refuge: Should We Save the Salton Sea?” *High County News*. 19 June 2000. hcn.org/issues/181/5865.

Niles, Natalie. “Exploring the Toxic Ruins of a Forgotten Resort.” Blog post. Theme Park Insider. Sept. 2019. themeparkinsider.com/flume/201909/7028/.

Olalde, Mark. "Calif. Democrats Decry Federal Inaction in Congress' First Hearing on Salton Sea in 23 Years." *The Desert Sun.* 24 Sept. 2020. desertsun.com/story/news/environment/2020/09/24/california-democrats-lambast-federal-inaction-salton-sea-hearing/5854882002.

Otto, Rebekah. "Salton Sea." Atlas Obscura. 31 Jan. 2010. atlasobscura.com/places/salton-sea.

Perry, Tony. "Leonard Knight, Artist at Salvation Mountain, Dies at Age 82." *Los Angeles Times.* 11 Feb. 2014. latimes.com/local/lanow/la-me-ln-leonard-mountain-20140210-story.html.

Petty, Amber. "Popular Places That Are Now Ghost Towns." Grunge.com. 25 Dec. 2020. grunge.com/56251/popular-places-now-ghost-towns/?utm_campaign=clip.

Rylah, Juliet Bennett. "How the Salton Riviera Became an Abandoned Wasteland." Culture Trip. 04 Sept. 2017. theculturetrip.com/north-america/usa/california/articles/how-the-salton-riviera-became-an-abandoned-wasteland.

"The Salton Sea—Part 1: A Distillation of the West's Problems in Search of Solutions." Desert Dispatches/High & Dry: Dispatches from the Land of Little Rain. 21 Apr. 2015. desertdispatches.com/blog/2015/4/the-salton-sea-a-distillation.

"Salton Sea Description." Salton Sea Description. 03 Oct. 1997. sci.sdsu.edu/salton/Salton%20Sea%20Description.

Spiegelman, Ian, and -. "How the Salton Sea, Once a Leisure Destination, Became an Ecological Time Bomb." *Los Angeles Magazine.* 24 Sept. 2020. lamag.com/culturefiles/salton-sea-documentary.

Staff. "Leonard Knight Biography, Life & Quotes." The Art Story. 2014. theartstory.org/artist/knight-leonard/life-and-legacy.

Tracy, B. "Bombay Beach." Atlas Obscura. 14 June 2011. atlasobscura.com/places/bombay-beach.

Ulrich, Amanda. "As Slab City Grows, the Community of Outcasts, Squatters, and Desert Dwellers Grapples with the Cost of Its Unique Freedoms." Roadtrippers. 11 Feb. 2020. roadtrippers.com/magazine/slab-city-california-desert.

Zebulon. "Rest in Peace Charlie Russell." Blog post. Adventures in the Zone. 11 May 2011. zebulonspleen.blogspot.com/2011/05/rest-in-peace-charlie-russell.